THE FOOTPRINTS BOOK OF DAILY INSPIRATIONS

*From the creator of "Footprints" to you—
a year and a day of thoughtful reflections
on life, spirituality, and faith*

footprints

THE FOOTPRINTS BOOK OF DAILY INSPIRATIONS

MARGARET FISHBACK POWERS

C Collins

The Footprints Book of Daily Inspirations
© 2008 by Margaret Fishback Powers. All rights reserved.

Published by Collins, an imprint of HarperCollins Publishers Ltd

First edition

HarperCollins books may be purchased for educational, business, or sales promotional use through our Special Markets Department.

HarperCollins Publishers Ltd
2 Bloor Street East, 20th Floor
Toronto, Ontario, Canada
M4W 1A8

www.harpercollins.ca

Library and Archives Canada Cataloguing in Publication

Powers, Margaret Fishback
The footprints book of daily inspirations / Margaret Fishback Powers.

ISBN 978-1-55468-242-3

1. Devotional calendars. I. Title.

BV4811.P683 2008   242'.2   C2008-901844-3

DWF 9 8 7 6 5 4 3 2 1

Printed and bound in Canada
Beach image by Joe Drivas/Getty Images
Interior design by Sharon Kish

PREFACE

Each day offers us a new opportunity to take steps in the right direction, steps that enlighten, instruct, enrich, or improve us and others. In your daily walk, have you ever left behind a trail of footprints that you wished you could erase? Do not despair; we all have days like that. But today is a new day, one in which you can leave behind footprints that will make you proud.

For this book, I have carefully selected verses and thoughts that have had a direct influence on my daily life and decisions, words that have helped me form healthy habits, thought patterns, and conduct. You will find herein a variety of insightful or amusing thoughts, writings, sayings, and poems, along with quotes from family members or famous people who have inspired me.

I am grateful to my husband, Paul, a serious but witty poet with many one-liners, which come in handy in our work with children in The Little People's Ministry Association that we co-founded over 40 years ago. I would like to thank Heather MacGregor for her additions, and both my daughters, Christina Michelle and Paula Margaret, for their part in this inspirational collection. I also appreciate the concentrated efforts of Bruce Nuffer, who spent hours editing and proofing, and who has been most positive. My thanks go, too, to Lloyd Kelly of HarperCollins Publishers for his many years of trust and hope. His support and patient listening have greatly encouraged me many times over. And, finally, to everyone else at HarperCollins, including Noelle Zitzer, Allegra Robinson, Sharon Kish, Neil Erickson, Nita Pronovost, Shelley Tangney, Steve Osgoode, Emma Ingram, Leo MacDonald, Michael Guy-Haddock, Lori Richardson, and Sandra Leef.

To my readers, it is my hope that you will consider the daily thoughts written here and so begin your mornings on the right foot, which will then lead to a whole day of meaningful footprints.

—MARGARET FISHBACK POWERS
JULY 2008

FOOTPRINTS

One night I dreamed a dream
I was walking along the beach with my Lord.
Across the dark sky flashed scenes from my life.
For each scene, I noticed two sets
of footprints in the sand,
one belonging to me
and one to my Lord . . .

When the last scene of my life shot before me
I looked back at the footprints in the sand.
There was only one set of footprints.
I realized that this was at the lowest
and saddest times of my life.
This always bothered me
and I questioned the Lord
about my dilemma.

"Lord, you told me when I decided to follow You,
You would walk and talk with me all the way.
But I'm aware that during the most troublesome
times of my life there is only one set of footprints.
I just don't understand why, when I needed You most,
You leave me."

He whispered, "My precious child,
I love you and will never leave you
never, ever, during your trials and testings.
When you saw only one set of footprints
it was then that I carried you."

Many of us have a special regard for the gemstones that mark the month of our birth. January's gemstones, garnets, come in different colors and shapes. Carnations are the flowers of January, and they, too, come in a variety of colors. When you give carnations, you are said to be expressing affection, happiness, and deep love.

JANUARY

Gates can stop us in our tracks, but they can also be entry points to great beginnings. When you come upon a gate in your journey, it's up to you to open the latch, take that first step inside, and proceed toward your goals.

AT THE GATE OF THE YEAR

I said to the Man,
At the Gate of the Year:
"What light cans't thou lend,
to those entering here?
I never have traveled,
This pathway before,
Thy help and thy counsel,
I humbly implore.
How can I discover,
What lieth ahead,
That I may walk safely,
Wherever I tread?

—ADAPTED FROM THE POEM BY
MINNIE LOUISE HASKINS

When I wrote the poem most of you know as "Footprints," I originally entitled it "I Had a Dream." This was only a year after an illustrious man made a speech with nearly the same name, but I didn't consciously intend to reference his speech. After all, dreams are important in so many ways. Not only do they unfold while our minds are most unencumbered, they also help keep us going when life's obstacles seem insurmountable. Author Anaïs Nin once said that it is our dreams that pass into the reality of action, and from that action stems the dream again. What dreams are you holding on to? How can you turn them into action?

Children are a gift too great for us to fully comprehend. As parents, we must realize that their years with us pass so quickly and that we owe them the best we can provide. Cherished children have a better sense of who they are and who they can be.

LITTLE FINGERS

If you knew the little fingers,
pressed against the window pane,
would be cold and stiff tomorrow,
never trouble us again,
would the bright eyes of our darling
catch the frown upon your brow?
Would the prints of rosy fingers
vex us then, as they do now?

—AUTHOR UNKNOWN

It is no revelation that we live in a selfish world. But few people would describe themselves as selfish. Yet consider this: How often do we see others—or do we ourselves—get filled with joy at the success of others? When you learn of someone winning the lottery, is your first thought about how nice a turn his or her life just took, or is your first thought about how nice it would have been if you had won the money yourself? How easy is it for you to be happy at the success of others?

Times of solitude are really wonderful opportunities to find peaceful moments with the Almighty.

PRAYER FOR THOSE WHO LIVE ALONE

I live alone, dear Lord, stay by my side.
In all my daily needs be Thou my guide.
Grant me good health, for that indeed, I pray,
to carry on my work from day to day.
Keep pure my heart, my thoughts, my every
    deed.
Let me be kind, unselfish in my neighbor's
    need.
Spare me from fire, from flood, malicious
    tongues,
from thieves, from fear and evil ones.
If sickness or an accident befall,
then humbly, Lord, I pray,
hear Thou my call,
and when I'm feeling low,
or in despair, lift up my heart
and help me in my prayer.
I live alone dear Lord,
yet have no fear,
because I feel Your presence
ever near.

—AUTHOR UNKNOWN

As far as we know, the concept of paying it forward was first suggested by Benjamin Franklin in a letter he wrote to Benjamin Webb in 1784. It wasn't until 1951, however, that Robert A. Heinlein actually coined the phrase in his book *Between Planets.* Doing kindness to those around us—whether we know them or not—is a universal theme that transcends cultural boundaries or religious doctrines. Look for an opportunity today to pass on to another the good that has been done you in the past.

Heavenly Father, bless this day before us.
May this New Year find us to be more willing
   to do your will,
to serve you by doing kindness to our fellow
   man.
I ask this in your love.
Amen

—MFP

King David said "search me," "know me," "try me," and "see me."

Am I willing for you to search me today? To know me, know my heart, my life, even my thoughts day by day?

Then to "try me"? What will the results of this testing be?

"See me." Will you see things in me that displease you? Then "lead me" in the direction of your will for me!

Don't be too harsh with the one who errs,
nor judge with words or stone,
unless you are sure, yes, genuinely sure,
you have no errors of your own!

—MFP

How many times has someone asked you to wait just a minute? Or how many times have you said that you'll do something in just a minute? I wonder how much time we'd get back if we could add up all of those lingering minutes, never mind the fact that many times that minute turns into two or three, or more. Life happens one minute at a time. We should be sure not to waste time on things that we can't change and instead focus on the things we can improve.

I have only just a minute,
    just sixty seconds in it;
forced upon me—can't refuse it,
didn't seek it, didn't choose it;
but it's up to me to use it.
I must suffer if I lose it,
give account if I abuse it,
Just a tiny little minute,
but eternity is in it.

—AUTHOR UNKNOWN

It may seem like just a little thing, but I've always wondered why we don't put things back where they belong when we are finished with them. Instead, we tend to leave items where they were last used, believing that we will return and put them away later. If you get into the habit of putting away things when you are done using them, then you and everyone else will know where to find them the next time they are needed.

I expect to pass through this world but once.
   Any good therefore that I can do or any
   kindness that I can show to any fellow
   creature, let me do it now.
Let me not defer nor neglect it, for I shall not
   pass this way again.

—AUTHOR UNKNOWN

There is no power on earth great enough to stop the tide, and that principle operates all through life: What goes out comes in . . . love . . . hate . . . mercy . . . What we give, we get!

When he was nearly forty years old, a man heard that the average human life expectancy is seventy-seven years. After some figuring, he realized that we have roughly 4,000 Saturdays in our lives. And what's more, he found that he had only about 1,500 left! Deciding he needed a physical reminder of his remaining days so he would stop putting off things for the future, he went out and bought 1,500 marbles and placed them in a large container in his bathroom. Then, every Saturday, he would drop one marble into a jar. In this way, he challenged himself to begin living a life of significance, knowing that day by day his opportunity to make a positive difference in the lives of others was waning.

When your life is nearing its end, will you have remembered to spend your efforts in helping others, or will you regret that you put off too many things for a tomorrow that may never come?

Character is what develops in us as a result of training as children and hardships as adults. It is rarely a pleasant endeavor that forges new character in us since we usually avoid taking on difficulties voluntarily. Yet when difficulty is unavoidable, and we meet it with the tenacity to be bigger than the problems that face us, the maturity we gain guides us for the rest of our lives.

In a culture in which most people focus on tomorrow, living day to day is an exceptionally difficult skill to learn. But every day thousands of unemployed people are forced to fight their natural impulses to live for the future and focus on the challenge of finding work today.

No one would envy those who are put in this unfortunate position. But some who have passed through such a difficulty report that they gained a new appreciation for the everyday things they had, including their families and their health. Those who are able to glimpse this rainbow amidst such cloudy days are truly blessed.

*There is no free gate to anything worthwhile—
not to skill nor health, success nor friendship,
or even to the lasting love and respect of those
who are nearest and dearest to us. These are
the items that make up the best yearly income
that any human being can have, and the sum
of the income will be measured by the sum of
what we are willing to pay to get it.*

—PAUL L. POWERS

If you wouldn't write it and sign it, don't say it.
  —Earl Wilson

And let's go one step further: With the popularity of the Internet these days, writing whatever comes to mind is far too easy. There is a tendency to fire off an e-mail without letting issues settle to make sure we say only what is wise. Perhaps it seems naive to suggest that our friends and family don't need to know everything we are thinking, but really, do you want to know everything they are thinking?

We all know the feeling of wanting to vent at others when we feel wronged. For my part, I am grateful that my mind isn't quick enough to come up with all the verbal barbs I'd like to throw in the heat of the moment, especially since I understand the grief that usually comes when I do vent my anger. When all else fails and it's really difficult to keep my mouth shut, I remember the Bible verse that says that in being kind to our enemies we are heaping burning coals on their heads. I suppose it's not the most charitable thought I've ever had, but it is usually good enough to help me escape saying something I know I'll regret later!

If you your lips would keep from slips,
Five things observe with care:
Of whom you speak, to whom you speak,
And how and when and where.

—AUTHOR UNKNOWN

Someone once said, "If you think you are too small to do a big thing, try doing small things in a big way."

The book Random Acts of Kindness *was on the right track. If you regret that you may never get into the history books with your benevolence, aim to simply brighten someone's day. Drop candy onto a person's desk when he or she isn't looking and just enjoy the response.*
—HEATHER MACGREGOR

Many people, when asked what they want, reply that they just want to be happy. But happiness is an inward-focused desire. When we are children, we think that when we become adults, we'll be happy. As students, we think that once we graduate, we'll be happy. And on and on the cycle continues as we look forward to a new job, a new house, or retirement as the thing or event that will finally bring us happiness. But because happiness is a fleeting, inward-focused desire, it is impossible for us to capture it in a lasting form.

Really, joy is what we are seeking. Joy is a deeper experience resulting from an outward-focused life. By concentrating on things beyond ourselves, we are able to escape our self-centered preoccupation and connect with something that is greater than ourselves.

In their recent popular book, *You: Staying Young,* physicians Michael Roizen and Mehmet Oz tackle the issue of aging and how human beings can live longer. The authors describe aging not as a matter of avoiding disease but of learning to live with vitality. What is the key ingredient of living with vitality? Meditation. In short, when the body is under stress, it releases chemicals that add to the pressure on it. The vagus nerve then works to reduce the stress. However, when the body sends out too many stress signals, the vagus nerve effectively short-circuits the brain's power to discern all the stress information. Regardless of what you believe the practice can do for you, one thing now seems clear—meditation can aid the vagus nerve's function by relaxing your body and allowing more time for its functions to deal constructively with the stress that remains. And less stress can literally add years to your life.

Rest is not only very important for our physical lives but also most important for our spiritual lives. King David wrote, "Be still and know that I am God." Be *still*—be quiet, take it easy, and don't rush about. Have a quietness of heart and spirit in which you can sense God's presence. Enjoy the stillness and silence of the soul.

I'm sure that I must sound like an old fogey when I say this, but one lesson my life has taught me is that time is not my friend. So many of our regrets in life are related to not doing something we should have done when we had the time—we missed telling someone how we really felt, we missed getting the education we always wanted, we missed learning that coveted skill because we put it off until tomorrow. One day I intend to ask God why procrastination seems to be such a strong part of our human nature. But until that day, I will continue to struggle against time by doing what needs to be done as soon as possible.

It was a high counsel that I once heard given to a young person: "Always do what you are afraid to do."
—RALPH WALDO EMERSON

This is not one of Emerson's better known quotes, but it is an intriguing concept on which to meditate. Here Emerson acknowledges that it is in our nature to take the paths of least resistance—abstain from doing the difficult things or those that cause us discomfort. But in so doing, we miss out on many of the blessings and opportunities life presents us.

Learning to spend time alone each day in prayer can bring us closer to our Maker. Our prayer time is not meant to be spent asking what God can do for us but rather in becoming more aware of what he is doing in our lives.

THE PLACE OF PRAYER

There is a place where thou canst touch the eyes
Of blinded men to instant, perfect sight;
There is a place where thou canst say, "Arise"
To dying captives, bound in chains of night;
There is a place where thou canst reach the store
Of hoarded gold and free it for the Lord;
There is a place—upon some distant shore—
Where thou canst send the worker and the Word.
Where is that secret place—dost thou ask, "Where?"
O soul, it is the secret place of prayer!
—ALFRED, LORD TENNYSON

Today is the birthday of eighteenth-century Scottish poet Robert Burns. Burns is admired for many reasons, one being that he used his skill to make people aware of the blight and plight of poverty and class inequality. My favorite poem of his—and given its worldwide popularity, a favorite of scores of people—is this one, which epitomizes the burden of the downtrodden in society:

SELKIRK GRACE

Some hae meat and canna eat,
(Some have meat and cannot eat,)
and some wad eat that want it,
(and some would eat that want it,)
but we hae meat and we can eat,
(but we have meat and we can eat,)
and sae the Lord be thankit.
(and so the Lord be thanked.)

—ROBERT BURNS

You may have today to help change someone's life for the better. Will you do it?

I have no Yesterdays.
Time took them away;
Tomorrow may not be—
But I have today!

—PEARL Y. McGINNIS

I enjoy finding proof that our forefathers from centuries ago did not live so different a life from ours as we sometimes imagine.

Ability wins us the esteem of the true men; luck that of the people.
—François de La Rochefoucauld

The first month of the year has nearly come to an end. Now would be a great time to get started on something new!

When I was young I was amazed at Plutarch's statement that the elder Cato began at the age of eighty to learn Greek. I am amazed no longer. Old age is ready to undertake tasks that youth shirked because they would take too long.

—W. Somerset Maugham

As parents, we all have days when we reach the end of our rope with our children. I have found that keeping myself organized and setting routines and boundaries for children solve most of the daily problems. Failing that, grab another rope!

MORNING MEDITATION

When little things irk me,
and I grow impatient with my dear ones,
help me to know
how in a moment joy can take its flight,
and happiness is quenched in endless night.
Keep this thought with me all the livelong day,
that I may guard the harsh words I might say.
When I would fret and grumble fiery hot
at trifles that tomorrow are forgot
Let me remember, Lord, how it would be
if these, my loved ones, were not here with me.

—AUTHOR UNKNOWN

Sometimes we pray with our own motives in mind and not truly with the intention of altruism. If you have a request, it is always best to make it clearly known. After all, God already knows your motive.

SHE WANTED SNOW

The little girl was never forgetful of formal prayers, and she had been allowed the privilege of adding any original remarks that she saw fit. One night in mid-January, at the end of her prayer, she added a p.s.: "Dear Jesus, please send a blanket of soft snow to keep the little flowers warm through the winter."

Getting back into bed she said to her mother, "This time I fooled Him. I really want the snow so I can go on my new sled!"

—REVEREND LEROY GAGER

I recently read an article discussing how impressionable we all are and how susceptible we are to the power of suggestion. By way of example, the article discussed how yawning is contagious (as a matter of fact, I just yawned while writing this and thinking about the idea!). Yawning is so contagious, the article suggested, that even cats will yawn in response to a human yawn. (If you try it, let me know if it works.) As an experiment today, see how contagious your smiles are. Smile at ten people and note how many smile back. Then pat yourself on the back for brightening someone's day.

In the New Year there is a facelift you can perform yourself. It is guaranteed to improve your appearance the rest of the year. It is called a SMILE!

—AUTHOR UNKNOWN

The birthstone for February is amethyst, a type of quartz, which comes in colors ranging from pale lilac to black purple. It is often called the stone of peace and tranquillity.

February's flowers are violets, which are said to symbolize faithfulness, purity, and modesty.

FEBRUARY

The setting of my poem "Footprints" is the beach. It is a figurative place that represents a spot each of us has where we can best sit in silence to meditate, reflect, dream, and ponder. It is no surprise, then, that a revelation comes to the poem's narrator on the beach. It is in our silences that we most often hear the answers to our deepest questions and the advice that would guide our lives.

"He's a chip off the old block." "She's the spitting image of you." Our children usually resemble us physically in some way or other, but the similarity certainly doesn't end there. It's sometimes astonishing to hear what our children say and to see what they do—and it can be shocking when we realize that these are some of the same things that we have said and done!

A careful person I ought to be,
a little fellow follows me.
I do not dare to lead him astray,
for fear he'll go the selfsame way.
Not once can I escape his eyes,
whatever he sees me do he tries.
Like me he says he's going to be,
that little chap who follows me.
I must remember as I go,
through summer sun and winter snow
I'm molding for the years to be—
that little chap who follows me.

—AUTHOR UNKNOWN

When you set an example for someone in your life—a child, a friend, a coworker—what you do will always trump what you say.

The way to gain a good reputation is to endeavor to be what you desire to appear.
—SOCRATES

3 FEBRUARY

Clichés and platitudes are things that sound good but that we often dismiss without further thought. That's what I did when I first read the following quote from Henry David Thoreau: "Go confidently in the direction of your dreams. Live the life you have imagined." Initially my response was "Right. Try telling that to someone with cancer, or someone who is unemployed, or someone who lives in poverty." But as I considered that quote again during a difficult time in my life, when I was gradually realizing that I truly had no control over much of anything, it suddenly had meaning for me. I realized that the life I have imagined is more a matter of a state of mind than physical prosperity or success. In my discouraging times, I realize I can choose to appreciate my health, my safety, and my family, rather than taking them for granted. They are things that money cannot replace and things that in the end I would give anything to keep.

Keeping a positive outlook through difficult times can lead to unexpected opportunities and success. Not every one of us is born with this attribute, but we can learn to be positive people and set a good example of this, especially when we are with young children.

The men whom I have seen succeed best in life have always been cheerful and hopeful men, who went about their business with a smile on their faces and took the changes and chances of this mortal life like men, facing rough and smooth alike as they came.
—CHARLES KINGSLEY

The making of a man begins in his cradle.
—P. M. CALLAHAN

Always kiss your children
goodnight—even if they are asleep.

*You cannot lift your children to a higher level
than that on which you live yourself.*

—AUTHOR UNKNOWN

Imagine a political front-runner, or for that matter an office-mate, living by the rules quoted below. Make a difference in the world today—focus on one of these modern sins and refuse to commit it.

THE SEVEN MODERN SINS

Policies without principles
Pleasure without conscience
Wealth without work
Knowledge without character
Industry without morality
Science without humanity
Worship without sacrifice

—AUTHOR UNKNOWN

I know several successful salespeople who have to live with the stigma of being in a profession marred by the misconduct of their predecessors. Have you ever had the joy of meeting a salesperson who thinks about your needs before his or her commission? Whether shopping for insurance or shoes, I relish spending time with a salesperson who truly seems to care about me. There are not many stores to which people declare themselves loyal, but I will be a customer forever to those salespeople who have proven themselves to me.

Without a doubt the world needs love like a parched land needs water. Everyone can make a positive contribution to the peace of the world by following Jesus' injunction to love one another. On a more personal level, love can help your relationship with your neighbor or your family. It can even create an atmosphere conducive to swaying crowds or selling soap!

—PAUL L. POWERS

Nearly a century after William Shakespeare lived, William Penn founded the city of Philadelphia, whose name means "the city of brotherly love." He named it so because he envisioned the arca as a place where all people could live together in peace and harmony. The sentiment may be old, but the thought is still as important as ever.

Be devoted to one another in brotherly love. Honor one another above yourselves.
—ROMANS 12:10

Therefore, love moderately; long love doth so; Too swift arrives as tardy as too slow.
—WILLIAM SHAKESPEARE, *Romeo and Juliet*

9 FEBRUARY

While this proverb seems to contradict the advice of those who would encourage us to live each day as if it were our last, it actually reinforces it. Education improves the quality of our lives and shows stewardship of our bodies and minds. To gain knowledge not only helps us fulfill our potential every day, it allows us to enjoy our days to their fullest.

If you are planning for a year, sow rice;
If you are planning for a decade, plant trees;
If you are planning for a lifetime, educate people.

—CHINESE PROVERB

Theodore Roosevelt said, "Nobody cares how much you know until they know how much you care." Focus your attention on caring.

It's interesting to know that the more that I come to know, the more I realize how much I don't know.

He who knows not and knows he knows not—he is a child. Teach him.
He who knows and knows not that he knows—he is asleep. Wake him up.
He who knows not and knows not that he knows not—he is a fool. Shun him.
He who knows and knows he knows—he is wise. Follow him.

—OMAR KHAYYÁM

Helen Keller (1880–1968) was one of the most remarkable people ever to grace our planet. Although an illness left her deaf and blind at nineteen months, she nevertheless became an articulate spokesperson for the dignity of all people. Let her life remind you that we don't need to be perfect to do good things; we all have gifts that we can make the most of.

Believe, when you are most unhappy, that there is something for you to do in the world. So long as you can sweeten another's pain, life is not in vain.

—HELEN KELLER

Valentine's Day arouses thoughts of love. The heart has become a universal symbol for this day and for love itself.

Another symbol of love is India's Taj Mahal. In the seventeenth century, Emperor Shah Jahan had the magnificent structure built as a monument to his favorite wife, Mumtaz Mahal. For more than 350 years, the imposing mausoleum has moved people with its sheer beauty and the story of the love that inspired its construction. Buildings deteriorate and, in time, the Taj Mahal will be a ruin, nothing more than a beautiful memory. Our greatest testimony to love is the acts of compassion we perform toward those less fortunate than we are. These acts are more enduring and not subject to decay.

In studying history, I have been shocked by how short average lifespans were in the past. Yet despite a life expectancy of only thirty or forty years, previous generations accomplished great things before their early demise. When I reflect on this, a little saying I wrote long ago comes to mind: It is not *how long* you live but *for what* you live that counts.

Raytown, a difficult school district in Missouri, has a policy that is considered revolutionary. Raytown insists that its teachers maintain tough rules but that they temper them with grace to allow children to misstep boundaries without fear of overly harsh discipline. Strange that grace is considered so revolutionary.

Grace isn't a little prayer we chant before receiving a meal. It's a way to live.
—JACKIE WINDSPEAR

I find it so difficult to pack lightly when traveling, and the worst thing about it is that I bring clothes back home unworn and wrinkled. I now try not to pack as much, since traveling is so much easier with a lighter suitcase. The same is so true about life. We hang on to possessions that we will never need again, and, even worse, we hold on to memories and bad feelings that we should let go of. Make sure that you take the time to think about how you can lighten your load before you end up going through life just making your arms longer.

And really, how distressing would our midlife crises be if we already had plans in place for legacies to our children?

Broken or missing things take on a smaller significance when I am pouring myself into the spiritual growth of others. I've finally come to the conclusion that life is a journey. So pack lightly.

—P. M. CALLAHAN

Loving others is so important to fulfilling our potential as human beings that crimes of neglect are far worse than purely physical crimes because of the psychological trauma they cause their victims. But loving is hard—and scary. It is risky because our love can go unacknowledged, unrewarded, and even unwanted. But to become the fullest manifestations of ourselves, we must love others despite the risks.

'Tis better to have loved and lost,
Than never to have loved at all.
—ALFRED, LORD TENNYSON

When you have endeavored to live your life generously helping and giving to others, it is often difficult when you yourself must accept help. When you find yourself in a position of need, choose to allow others to experience the blessing that comes from giving, and let yourself be the tool through which that blessing comes.

STICK-TOGETHER FAMILIES

The stick-together families
Are happier by far
Than the brothers and the sisters
Who take separate highways are.
The gladdest people living
Are the wholesome folk who make
A circle at the fireside
That no power but death can break.
And the finest of conventions
Ever held beneath the sun,
Are the little family gatherings
When the busy day is done.

—EDGAR GUEST

A person can have no better epitaph than
that which is inscribed in the hearts of their
families.

—AUTHOR UNKNOWN

Oh, I wish I'd known to say this when I heard children ask, "Why do I need to go to school?"

Bear in mind that the wonderful things you learn in your schools are the work of many generations. All this is put in your hands as your inheritance in order that you may receive it, honor it, add to it, and one day faithfully hand it on to your children.
—ALBERT EINSTEIN

As I have matured, I have seen that my temptations have also matured. Petty thoughts and notions no longer tempt me as they did in my youth. Now my temptations are of a far more abstract nature. One temptation I have considered at length is the desire to hold back forgiveness from someone who needs it. I no longer subscribe to the notion that forgiving and forgetting are two sides of the same coin; some wrongs done to me are simply too painful to forget. Rather, these days I reflect on forgiveness as defined by Anne Lamott in *Further Thoughts on Faith:* "Forgiveness is not wanting to hit back." Today, if you struggle with forgiving someone because of grandiose thoughts of also forgetting the wrong, see if you can move the goal a little closer—just see if you can refrain from wanting to hurt the person back.

Did it ever strike you that goodness is not merely a beautiful thing, but by far the most beautiful thing in the whole world? So that nothing is to be compared for value with goodness, that riches, honour, power, pleasure, learning, the whole world and all in it, are not worth having in comparison with being good; and the utterly best thing for a man is to be good, even though he were never to be rewarded for it.

—Charles Kingsley

We all know that our society is obsessed with looking beautiful, so I find solace in these words of an actress who can keep her momentary successes in perspective. . . .

There is so much more than that little space from 14 to 40. And if you cut that off and begin to believe that you are not good past a certain age, then you end up scared and insecure and afraid. That is definitely not beautiful.

—RENEE RUSSO

In the orphanages of many foreign countries, the infants so far outnumber the workers that the children learn quickly that no one is going to take care of their needs when they cry. This foundational learning in infants is so strong that children adopted into a loving home even within their first year may revert to infantile behavior years later. Some sociologists explain that these children, now feeling assured of the unconditional love of their new parents, feel the need to go back and experience what it is like to be loved and cared for as babies.

Too often we underestimate the power of a touch, a smile, a kind word, a listening ear, an honest compliment, or the smallest act of caring, all of which have the potential to turn a life around.

—LEO BUSCAGLIA

The longer I live, the more I realize the impact of attitude on life. Attitude, to me, is more important than facts. It is more important than the past, the education, the money, than circumstances, than failure, than successes, than what other people think or say or do. It is more important than appearance, giftedness or skill. It will make or break a company . . . a church . . . a home. The remarkable thing is we have a choice every day regarding the attitude we will embrace for that day. We cannot change our past . . . we cannot change the fact that people will act in a certain way. We cannot change the inevitable. The only thing we can do is play on the one string we have, and that is our attitude. I am convinced that life is 10% what happens to me and 90% how I react to it. And so it is with you . . . we are in charge of our Attitudes.

—CHUCK SWINDOLL

Which of us, when struck back, says, "Okay then, you got me good. Now we're even." No, we typically feel that the other person's response was unwarranted, thus meriting our striking back yet again. Some people, and even countries, fight feuds long after anyone remembers their instigation. Is it any wonder that there isn't really such a thing as "getting even"?

Peace is not merely a distant goal that we seek but a means by which we arrive at that goal.
—MARTIN LUTHER KING JR.

The more we argue with others—or disagree, as we may prefer to think of it—the more arrogant we become. When we argue, we are saying we are more knowledgeable than those with whom we are speaking. And, of course, the reputation a person like this gains is that of "know-it-all."

The more arguments you win, the less friends you will have.

—AMERICAN PROVERB

There is a story about a woman who complained that her burdens were too heavy to bear. One night she had a vivid dream in which the Lord appeared and relieved her of her cross. He led her into a large field filled with crosses of every conceivable size and shape. He said, "Everyone must bear a cross alone. Since your cross is more than you can bear, go and choose the one you think is not too difficult yet worthy of your strength and courage." The woman went into the field and searched diligently for a cross. At last she chose one and said, "This is it. It is neither too heavy nor too light." So the Lord gave it to her. When she picked it up . . . lo, it was her own cross, the very one she had given to the Lord.

It is easy to become myopic about our own difficulties, and become blind to the difficulties of others. A cure for discouragement when life seems too hard is to find someone whose burdens seem too heavy for them and offer to lend a hand. Lend an ear. Send a card. Entering into their burdens not only eases their difficulty but takes some of the sting out of our own heartaches.

March's stone is aquamarine, a refreshing shade of sea-blue. This month's flowers are daffodils, which represent respect, and jonquils, which stand for sympathy.

MARCH

Every now and then, someone tells of an imaginary or presupposed time when we are standing before God at the end of our lives, watching a replay of all the good and bad things we've done. In "Footprints," I relied on a version of this imagery that is often overlooked. The timing of the poem is actually a later day, when the narrator is walking with God, watching scenes from her life as it plays out in a dramatic presentation in the sky. It may not be theologically correct that this is how we will be judged at the world's end, but I do believe we will be accountable for all we have said and done. Imagining such a test serves as a fearful reminder of the importance of my actions, but it also serves as a comfort as I am reminded that God sees every good thing we do as well.

I have often witnessed other people performing their life's work doing jobs for which I have neither the skill nor the passion, and I am comforted that they are called to their particular roles. I realize how important so many occupations are, and I appreciate people carrying out their work with vigor. As for my work, my father has sometimes told me that he cannot imagine a job more mundane than writing! Thank goodness we do not all share the same passions.

Life is like a band. We need not all play the same part, but we must play in harmony.

—AUTHOR UNKNOWN

John Lennon's song "Beautiful Boy" contains a very powerful line about life. The message is that no matter how much we try to plan our lives, the way they unfold is largely beyond our control or imagining. Life simply *happens* to you, regardless of all attempts to plot it out. Reflecting on the truth of that sobering thought is a wonderful reminder to me to appreciate each day as an end unto itself. If it's raining or snowing, or if I am downhearted, those words help me appreciate today for what it is, and to know that every hour is a gift.

A pendulum travels much, but it only goes a tick at a time. . . . We may live another fifty years, but we only live a day at a time. Therefore, we need not forestall the future, but simply "do the next thing."

—PAUL L. POWERS

I TOOK A TRAIN

I took a train one day to see
    if I could get away from me.
Though swift and far the engine sped—
    myself went hurrying on ahead.
I hurried through a secret door—
    myself had entered there before.
I went into a room to hide—
    myself already was inside.
However fast and far I flee,
    I cannot get away from me.

—MFP

We get so busy in our lives and cram them so full that there is seldom time to do all we want to in a day. The next time you are contemplating what is not going to get done, do yourself a favor—make sure you don't eliminate time for yourself. Not only does taking time for ourselves help ensure our physical health, it also helps us stay in touch with our deepest needs and desires.

If you ever want to feel blessed with the privilege of witnessing purity, ask a child to give thanks for the food at your next meal; the younger the child, the more honest and unpretentious the dialogue. We were invited to our daughter's home for Mother's Day. Her husband, a pastor, asked our granddaughter to bless the food. She replied, "It's been blessed already. It's all leftovers!"

OK, truth time. One big pet peeve of mine is people referring to children as our future. It's as if kids are considered of no account while they are young, but we should care for them because they will one day be in charge. Hello? Children are *part* of our world now. They are members of our churches now. Do not respect them only because of what they might mean to us in the future but for what they mean to us today.

When I approach a child, he inspires in me two sentiments: tenderness for what he is and respect for what he may become.
—LOUIS PASTEUR

There is freedom in accepting that we cannot achieve complete goodness on our own. No amount of our own effort can ever lead us to live lives of complete purity. As humans we have limitations, weaknesses, flaws, and impurities that prevent us from becoming truly good on our own. However, because of a thing called grace, we are allowed to misstep and yet remain in good standing with others. Regardless of your spiritual vantage point, grace is an amazing thing—it cannot be earned, it is given freely. Are you a giver of grace?

Amidst all the moaning about our world's ills, I seldom hear talk of a serious problem: the grievous absence of friends. In our disjointed and overly busy world, it seems many people don't have the opportunity for friendships. And yet there are few blessings in life equal to that of close friends, others with whom we can share our burdens without fear of reprisals or grudges. If you have close friends, thank God, and them, for their friendship.

When I kneel before your altar,
I can feel your presence there.
The load of care and sorrow
seems much easier to bear.
I am grateful for your mercies and love.
Amen

—MFP

George Müller, a native of Prussia, was born on September 27, 1805. His life was significant in that he became the greatest "father of the orphans" in all history. On March 5, 1834, he formed the Scriptural Knowledge Institution for Home and Abroad with the goal of aiding Christian schools and missionaries, and distributing the Bible.

On October 7, 1829, George Müller married Ashley Down. Together, they founded the great Ashley Down Orphanage in Bristol, England, which has become famous throughout the world. This man of incredible faith and prayer went to be with his Maker on March 10, 1889.

Harsh words, like chickens, love to stray
but they come home to rest each day.
If you have angry words to say—
stop and think!

The world will judge you by your deeds;
they can be flowers fair or weeds.
Before you plant those tiny seeds—
stop and think!

God gave us each a heart for song;
a brain to reason right from wrong.
So, when temptation gets too strong—
stop and think!

—HEATHER KAITLYN BARCLAY

In *The Family Circus* (which, according to King Features Syndicate, is the most syndicated comic strip in history), there is often a gremlin character named "Not Me." In a wonderful stroke that displays his recognition of our shortcomings as humans, the artist, Bill Keane, uses this character to reveal our natural tendency to disavow our own culpability in all sorts of mistakes and problems. And though the character is couched in humor, Keane is acutely aware of our desire to consider ourselves blameless.

A church is no more to be blamed for the bad people in it than a hospital is to be blamed for the sick ones that are in it.

—AUTHOR UNKNOWN

We purchased a pair of "farmer" coveralls with a pliers pocket on the right leg for a godson in the UK. We asked if he knew what it was for. "Yep, it's for keeping my cell phone in" was his reply. While we laughed, I thought about how often I have closed the door to some new perspective or way of thinking because I assumed there was no valid way of looking at something besides my own. It's a good reminder—just because we've always done it one way doesn't mean we always have to do it that way.

We are a reflection of God—created in his image. Our emotions are a mere glimpse of our Father's. We read about God's love and tenderness, his sorrow and anger, but what about his laughter? His humor? Humor is a part of who we are and it comes from God himself. Because of our sinful human nature, humor can become twisted and perverted, but in its purest form, is there anything more delightful than a child's laughter, a puppy chasing its tail, or a good clean joke? As dark as this world can be, there is humor all around us. We need to remember to lighten up a bit and not take ourselves too seriously!

—ASHLEY J. TAYLOR

Let's make this month better in every way by forgetting the things that are behind and remembering all the ways that the Lord led you. You know what they say . . . "Success comes in cans; failures in can'ts," so grab a can opener, and with it, you will find success!

It's day number seventy-five in the New Year (unless it's a leap year!). If you made a resolution to accomplish something (ahem, exercise?), are you keeping your promise? If you haven't made any headway toward your goal yet, why not start fresh today?

St. Patrick, the patron saint of Ireland, was born around AD 385. His birthplace has been the subject of heated debate for centuries. Early Irish tradition says he died in AD 461 on March 17. Green is associated with St. Patrick's Day because it is the color of spring, Ireland, and the shamrock. Spring is just around the corner now, when flowers will bloom, and everything will be green once again.

In the UK, Mother's Day, or "Mothering Sunday," is not a fixed day; it falls on the middle Sunday in Lent. Having enjoyed Mother's Day as a daughter, a mother, and a grandmother for many years, I hurt for all those who have never had this opportunity. If you know someone who doesn't have a mother to thank this year, or if you know a mother whose children are unable to show their appreciation, play the role of both mother and child. Tell those without their mothers in their lives something they would have loved to hear from their mothers—how proud they would have been, or that the world is a better place because of their gift of a child. For those whose children have passed on or are otherwise out of touch, let that mum know how much you appreciate her sacrifice. After all, parenting is not the same thing as mothering.

Pray daily, maybe just after reading this daily inspiration. Pray for things to change for the better, even if you think there is no way that some things can ever improve. . . . Who knows, you may be happily surprised!

The power of prayer has never been tried to its full capacity. . . . If we want to see mighty wonders of divine power and grace wrought in the place of weakness, failure, and disappointment, let us answer God's standing challenge.

—J. Hudson Taylor

"Call to me and I will answer you and tell you great and unsearchable things you do not know."

—Jeremiah 33:3

Have you ever wondered what makes the wind blow? Some days it's so strong, and other days there's not a breath of air. Well, it has something to do with atmospheric pressure. Regardless of the real explanation, I know that there's almost nothing I hate more than a cold or damp March wind. However, we all need a little wind beneath our wings now and then, to push us on to greater heights.

True courage is like a kite;
a contrary wind raises it higher.
—JOHN PETIT-SENN

Blow old March wind,
blow, blow, blow,
make the arms of the windmill go.
Flutter the clothes on the clothesline high
and whisk all the kites
right up in the sky.
—ANCIENT CELTIC SAYING

Even in a formal definition, wisdom is only lightly associated with knowledge, and is clearly distinct from it. Some see wisdom as a quality that even children can possess. Check your level of wisdom today and consider Plato's definition as a challenge: "Wisdom is knowledge about good and the courage to act accordingly."

Knowledge is not the same as wisdom; wisdom is the application of knowledge.
—HEATHER KAITLYN BARCLAY

We often end up being the answers to our own prayers. For whatever reason, God seems to work on this earth in partnership with us, and prayer is our main communication channel. When we pray about something, "God, don't you care?!" often the answer is, "Yes, I care, and I've chosen you to demonstrate that care."

—PHILIP YANCEY

A successful lawyer was visiting a farm and asked the farmer, "Why don't you hold up your head in the world as I do?" The farmer answered, "See that field of grain? Only the heads that are empty stand up. Those that are filled are the ones that bow low."

—CLARENCE HENRY FISHBACK

It's true that children grow up too fast. We always seem to be so busy with life that it can be challenging to spend enough quality time with our kids. However, try to think of parenting the same way you would think about your investments. Every minute, hour, or day that you spend with your child will bear "interest" down the road.

"Parental wisdom," says a bachelor, "consists of bringing up your children so someone else will like them besides you."

—WAYNE WELCH

When it seems that people in charge have taken on too much and need a helping hand running an event or performing their regular tasks, be careful when taking on their duties. When you put an *I* in the word *run,* you can sometimes *ruin* things for everyone. We often think that we can manage things better, especially when we see someone in a leadership position having difficulty. Kindly ask first how you can help. I'm sure he or she will be most grateful!

*Throughout the ages
no nation has ever had
a better friend
than the mother
who taught her children to pray.*

—MFP

The best of men and the most earnest workers will make enough mistakes to keep them humble. Thank God for mistakes, take courage, and don't give up. Remember, it is better to make a mistake and learn from it than to never try to learn something new. Be courageous and try something new today!

Constant transition has finally made me realize that this earth is not my home, not my permanent residence. My life in this world is but a blink, a precursor to eternity in heaven, where I will never have to move again. All the stuff I accumulate and repeatedly pack and unpack is temporal. The only things that truly last are God, the Word of God, and human souls.

—P. M. CALLAHAN

I've started putting together scrapbooks for each of my kids, and they love it! My way of retaining memories and "important stuff" is to keep it all contained in one or two books for each child and to work on the project twice a month . . . rain or shine. Like many mothers, I recorded *everything* about my first child, just as my mother had done, but by the time my daughter arrived, I scaled down to recording only major events.

My life is always so fast paced and sometimes confusing that I need a peaceful, quiet, and calming place to relax and catch my breath. Clutter doesn't soothe my soul, and it always takes me twice as long to find something than if it had been in the right place in the first place.

—P. M. CALLAHAN

Being a winner doesn't always come naturally. But if you make your best effort to be a winner, good things will naturally come to you.

A Winner is always part of the answer.
A Winner always has a program.
A Winner says "Let me do it for you."
A Winner sees an answer for every problem.
A Winner says "It may be difficult but it is
*   possible."*
A Winner chooses what to say.
A Winner makes it happen.

—ADAPTED FROM "WINNERS VS.
LOSERS" (AUTHOR UNKNOWN)

Is there something that you have been procrastinating about because it doesn't seem fair? Almost any job can be twice as hard to complete if you have the wrong attitude. There will always be duties that you don't want to undertake for one reason or another. If you go about work with a cheerful heart, you may be surprised how easy the job was after all.

Watch your attitude toward the thing that troubles you! Your attitude may hurt you more than the thing.

—DR. BARRY MOORE

April's gemstone is the diamond, and the month's flowers are the daisy, which symbolizes innocency and purity, and the sweetpea, which stands for delicacy, blissfulness, or curiosity.

APRIL

"For each scene, I noticed two sets of footprints in the sand, one belonging to me and one to my Lord."

In "Footprints," this passage is my way of emphasizing the fact that our journeys with God must happen in isolation. We are wise to listen to the advice of other travelers who have walked in life ahead of us, but no amount of advice or friendship can change the fact that our spiritual lives are a journey upon which each of us must set out with our own dedication to its pursuit.

Flowers and smiles both need to be shared often. After all, the most beautiful smiles are made with *two lips.*

What sunshine is to flowers, smiles are to humanity.

—JOSEPH ADDISON

When a circumstance or situation threatens to make me unhappy, I like to remember this African proverb, "It is better to be happy than to be the king."

The most powerful king on earth is wor-king;
the laziest king on earth is shir-king;
the worst king on earth is smo-king;
the wittiest king on earth is jo-king;
the quietest king on earth is thin-king;
the thirstiest king on earth is drin-king;
the noisiest king on earth is tal-king.
—HEATHER KAITLYN BARCLAY

We don't have to wait until we are asked to do something or to help someone out. It never hurts to just go ahead and offer your help when you see a need and are able to assist.

The world is waiting for somebody,
waiting and watching today—
somebody to lift and strengthen,
somebody to shield and stay.
Do you thoughtfully question, "Who?"
'Tis you, my friend, 'tis you.

—AUTHOR UNKNOWN

There is a balancing act we must perform when we consider what others think of us. It's popular to say we do not care what others think, and there is some wisdom in this attitude. But because people's perceptions create their reality, we should not simply dismiss criticism directed at us without carefully considering what truth the comments may hold.

Seeing ourselves as others see us wouldn't do much good because most of us wouldn't believe what we saw anyhow.

—PAUL L. POWERS

Five-year-old Max was running in the playground when suddenly he stopped and leaned against the wall, breathing heavily. His nana asked, "Are you all right?" His reply was, "Yep, just lost my breath." She asked if this had happened before. "It's OK, Nana. I found it the last time, too."

I feel sad when I encounter a child who has had to grow up too fast. As children, we have a wonderful determination that most of us lose as we age. Ask a roomful of children if they can sing. You'll have them all belting out whatever tunes first come to their minds. Ask them if they can dance, and they'll whirl around you until they fall down. But ask a roomful of adults the same questions, and you'll get embarrassed comments about how singing or dancing isn't really their forte. How do we lose the self-recrimination that prevents us from enjoying so many things?

Our children's Irish nanny would always say: "Find a penny, pick it up, and all the day you'll have good luck!"

George Müller shares the value of a penny. He told the story of how a lady put two pence in the orphanage house box saying, "It is only a trifle, but I must give it for the orphans." It so happened that that very day, a penny was needed to make up the amount of money necessary to buy bread! The next day, a single penny was needed to fill out the dinner menu. Thanks to the lady's humble contribution, the orphans had enough to eat.

We can all be one sent.

—HEATHER MACGREGOR

Do you have friends with whom you are so close that you don't have to clean your house every time they come over? It is so comforting to know that certain people know you so well they are not turned off by a little clutter. Are you that kind of friend to others?

Believe it or not, I do enjoy useless things, but only if they are beautiful and somehow speak soft soothing images to my mind. I want friends who enter my home to relax, not feel swamped or overwhelmed, about to be jumped on by a stack of books or papers, or mugged by pillows or bags. I want my home to reflect me—put together, but definitely lived in!

—P. M. CALLAHAN

Friends, like pianos, need frequent tuning.

You are in the right key when you sing the praises of others.

—HEATHER MACGREGOR

Those of us who have a close relationship with a sister are so fortunate to have someone we can share laughs, tears, and quiet moments with in a special way that might not be possible with anyone else.

There's the wonderful love of a beautiful maid,
the love of a staunch true man,
the love of a baby who's unafraid—
all have existed since time began.
But the most wonderful love,
the Love of all loves,
even greater than the love for Mother,
is the infinite, tenderest, passionate love
of one dear sister for the other!

—AUTHOR UNKNOWN

I t is true that our words can bring healing or desolation to others. But I think that the people who know and love me the most are the ones who best understand my silence.

Each word is a gem
from the celestial mines,
a sunbeam from the holy heaven
where holy sunlight shines.
                    —HORATIO BONAR

I once went through a time when I had a lot of trouble getting to sleep. After several nights, I realized that during the days, I was finding no quiet time to pray and meditate. When I finally lay down at night and had no distractions, my mind would seize on all of the *to dos* I had ignored all day. It was not a pleasant time for me, but it served as a good lesson in the importance of maintaining a quiet time during my waking hours.

It is good to listen carefully to what others say and observe carefully what others do. But it is essential that we think carefully when reading, as the written word can sometimes speak volumes to a listening heart.

Except a living man there is nothing more wonderful than a book! A message to us from the dead—from human souls whom we never saw, who lived, perhaps, thousands of miles away. Yet these, in those little sheets of paper, speak to us, amuse us, terrify us, teach us, comfort us, open their hearts to us as brothers. . . .

—CHARLES KINGSLEY

You can't always see the flaw in a bridge until it falls down or the flaw in a good man's character until he meets with temptation.

One of the most inspiring times of the year for me is Easter, which falls on a Sunday, usually between March 22 and April 25. People celebrate Easter according to their beliefs and their religious denominations. Christians commemorate Good Friday as the day that Jesus Christ died and Easter Sunday as the day that he was resurrected. Protestant settlers brought to the United States the custom of a sunrise service, a religious gathering at dawn on Easter Sunday.

The Easter egg symbolizes fertility and new life. The beautiful picture book *Easter Eggs for Anya* explains many of the Ukranian traditions surrounding Easter eggs. In medieval times, eggs were traditionally given to the servants at Easter. In Germany, eggs were given to children, along with other gifts.

One of the greatest ways to keep ourselves safe from potential disaster in this world is to understand the nature of the lies our culture tells us. One way our society encourages us to do wrong is to make the safe things in life appear boring or unsatisfying and to make the dangerous or forbidden things seem desirable. Are there temptations in your life to do something that your better judgment urges you to avoid?

In the entry for April 1, I discussed how in "Footprints" there is an underlying philosophy about how each of us must take our spiritual journeys alone. However, this is not entirely the case, since every true search for God results in finding him, and in finding him we have a traveling companion for the rest of our lives.

God is before me; He will be my guide;
God is behind me, no ill betide;
God is beside me, to comfort and cheer;
God is around me, so why should I fear?
—HEATHER KAITLYN BARCLAY

18

It is incalculable how much previous generations have done to make life easier for those that have followed. They have paved the way for us with innovation and grand conveniences, laws to protect the innocent, and civil liberties to encourage what is right. Some choose to ignore these advances, some even work against them, and others modify and improve them. I often hear people say, "There's nothing like the good old days." I have yet to see any of these people make an effort to do without the great things that we have today, so things must be getting better.

A home-schooling family I know received a microscope in the mail one day. They immediately turned it on and began looking at everything they could think of that might be made clearer by seeing it so enlarged. They spent a wonderful afternoon marveling at the wonder of creation hidden in microscopic detail. Today, stop somewhere just to look at the world around you and see what you can notice. Make a mental note of the things you realize you have taken for granted lately, and be thankful that you live in such a wonderful and complex world.

During a ministry trip to Germany a number of years ago, we read in a Swiss newspaper about the tragic accident of three visiting students who were killed in a fall over a precipice. Lacking knowledge of the surrounding mountain formation, and having little skill and experience, they came to a disastrous end when attempting a hazardous ascent. The paper stated they foolishly undertook a venture without a professional guide!

Sometimes we are just as foolish. We embark on our life's journey without our guide. Remember, in all ways, know, recognize, and acknowledge him.

I think that there is nothing more amazing than natural beauty in any form. The simplest, most plentiful things found in nature—a blade of grass, a drop of rain—cannot be created by human hands.

To gild refined gold, to paint the lily,
To throw a perfume on the violet,
To smooth the ice, or add another hue
Unto the rainbow, or, with taper-light,
To seek the beauteous eye of heaven to garnish,
Is wasteful and ridiculous excess.
                              —WILLIAM SHAKESPEARE,
                                              King John

Someone once asked Francis of Assisi how he was able to accomplish so much. He replied, "This may be why: The Lord looked down from heaven and said, 'Where can I find the weakest, littlest man on earth?' Then He saw me and said, 'I've found him. I will work through him, and he won't be proud of it. He'll see that I am only using him because of his insignificance.'"

Francis of Assisi had a handle on the knowledge that we can all be used to do good, no matter how inadequate we may feel, and sometimes even *because* we feel inadequate. When you are feeling low, remember that there is a long history of the greatest things being accomplished by the unlikeliest of people.

Here's some financial advice that the years have taught me. Lend to others what you can afford to never see again. If the money is returned, which is usually the case, then you are even; if not, then you have already written it off and won't find yourself in a financial crisis.

I once had money and a friend;
of either, thought I store.
I lent my money to my friend
and took his word therefore.
I sought my money from my friend,
which I had wanted long.
I lost my money and my friend;
now was that not a wrong?

—AUTHOR UNKNOWN

We may not always feel this way, but we *are* blessed! We are blessed with things that we may take for granted from time to time, such as love, friendships, an abundance of food, a home, and, most of all, a God above who watches over us and loves us.

I cannot find a truer word,
nor better, to address you!
Nor song, nor poem I have written,
is sweeter than, "God bless you."

God bless you! Thus I've wished you
all that Christian joy possesses,
for there can truly be no joy
unless, indeed, God blesses.

God bless you! So I breathe a charm
lest grief's dark night oppress you,
for how can sorrow bring you harm,
if it's God's way to bless you.

And so through all your earthly days
may shadows touch you never,
but if they should, God's blessing
will keep you safe forever.

—AUTHOR UNKNOWN

Isn't it amazing and wonderful that we are all born unique? It's inconceivable how such a miracle is even possible considering there are more than 6 billion people alive at this very point in time—and not one of them is just like you!

The child must know that he is a miracle,
that since the beginning of the world there
hasn't been, and until the end of the world
there will not be, another child like him.
—PABLO CASALS

I think that a pastor can use almost anything as material for a sermon. My husband had just gotten a new white shirt. He was wearing this shirt as the worship team gathered around the piano to go over some music. One of the team members asked my husband what was on his shirt; he looked down and realized that he had spilled coffee with cream down the front of it. Since I carry a Tide to Go stick in my purse, I quickly rubbed it over the huge stain. Within seconds, it was gone! The shirt was spotless and ready for the morning service!

Later in the service, my husband reflected on what had happened earlier with his white shirt. "It's a reminder of what Christ has done for us. We come to him in desperation, knowing that there is nothing we can do on our own to remove the stain of sin." Every time I use my "miraculous" Tide to Go stick, I will be reminded of the real miracle Christ has performed in my life.

—ASHLEY J. TAYLOR

I was privileged to grow up in a family in which reading and writing were the accepted norm. Our home library was always filled with excellent reading materials, including Bibles—extra ones, in case a visitor needed one.

Throughout my secondary school years, I suffered eye strain, so my dear mother would take an hour out of her busy day to read aloud to me the classics or a novel that was prescribed reading for the school year. She had incredible expression and inflection in her voice, and I miss it to this day. Those were some of my most precious moments with my mum, and they formed my "literary character."

Through reading *Pride and Prejudice*, I came to feel I knew Jane Austen so well that I was completely at home in her house (now a museum) in England. For me, Lizzy Bennet came alive, and I imagined her being wooed by Mr. Darcy, a man of great wealth. Lizzy, at first thinking Darcy very arrogant, rejects his love. Later, she discovers how kind and thoughtful he has been to others. Finally, she realizes she has misjudged him and agrees to marry him.

A reminder: First impressions sometimes lead to wrong conclusions.

*Any fool can find fault, but it takes a man
with a great heart to discover good in others
and speak of that good.*

—PAUL L. POWERS

For the life of me, I cannot figure out why calling someone a square is pejorative, unless it's because we know we would find it difficult to live such a disciplined life.

I know someone whom others consider square. He's a strong, polite, God-fearing young fellow who admits freely that he prays, weeps for joy, plays with little kids, kisses his mother, goes to his dad for advice, and thinks old folks are smart. He wears clothes that fit him, puts savings in the bank, has his hair neatly groomed, likes school, can't imitate all the television comics, avoids dirty discussions about sex—he even blushes. He goes to church regularly, drives within the speed limit, is in bed by 11 p.m., doesn't smoke, and expects wholesomeness in girls.

I think the world would be a much better place if we had a few more squares in it!

Now and then I hear someone say, "I don't know how to pray." And to be honest, I think even many of those who feel they *do* know how to pray often have a very narrow view of what praying is. Prayer is simply talking to God. Since he knows what our spirits are saying, even when we do not know ourselves, even the heart's happiness at seeing a sunrise—when we recognize God made it—is itself a praise to him. When we ask others to pray for us, we are letting it be known that we wish God to recognize our needs, and he does. So if you sometimes feel you can't pray—or don't know how—rest assured: your reflective concerns or praises are prayers in themselves.

HEART TIME

The while she darns her children's socks
she prays for the little stumbling feet.
Each folded pair within its box
fits faith's bright sandals, sure and fleet.

While washing out, with mother's pains
small dusty suits and socks and slips,
she prays that God may cleanse the stains
from little hearts and hands and lips.

Oh, busy ones, whose souls grow faint,
whose tasks seem longer than the day?
It doesn't take a cloistered saint
to find a little time to pray.

—AUTHOR UNKNOWN

The precious emerald is the birthstone for the month of May. It is sometimes referred to as "green stone" because of its color. Emeralds are available in many shapes, including cabochon and dome, and can even be carved. May's flower, the lily of the valley, represents humility, sweetness, and a return of happiness.

MAY

In "Footprints," there is a brief moment of reflection at the heart of the poem—it is a time when the narrator looks back at the events of her life. It is often difficult, sometimes even impossible amidst our present concerns, to predict how our current circumstances will affect our future. Looking back at the route we've traveled is important in understanding how the events of our lives have made us into the people we are.

At a seniors' residence, a group of elderly people were talking. One said, "Sometimes I go to the fridge but can't remember if I'm taking food out or putting it away." The next person added, "Sometimes when I'm at the foot of the stairs, I can't remember if I am coming down or getting ready to go up." A third person knocked on the wooden table and said, "I'll never have those problems, but somebody's at the door. . . ."

When Time who steals our years away shall
    steal our pleasures too,
the mem'ry of the past will stay
and half our joys renew.

—Thomas More

A church organist attempted to play the instrument, but no sound came from it. So the church service had to start without the direction of the organist. The problem was located, and the repairman, a member of the church, figured the organ would be functioning by the time the pastor completed the morning prayer. The usher slipped the pastor a note that said, "The power will be back on after you pray."

Prayer is the contemplation of the facts of life from the highest point of view.
—RALPH WALDO EMERSON

It can be a struggle between our hearts and our heads when we look in the mirror and notice those wrinkles that weren't there just a few years back. We all know we age, and we know what is going to happen to our bodies. But it usually isn't helpful to think those thoughts in the face of our hearts' groaning at our lost youth. But, truly, it is our souls that grow more and more attractive each year. The beauty that comes from the wisdom of age is a wonderful and hard-earned trophy. Next time you are dismayed at how fast time goes by, think about the speed at which you are becoming more beautiful!

When the *Titanic* was built, it was called the "unsinkable ship." However, the world soon learned that this was a misnomer, for on April 14, 1912, the vessel sank after hitting an iceberg. People had been lulled into a false sense of security. Over 1,500 people lost their lives. With God in the ship of your life, as your captain, you are truly "unsinkable," no matter how severe the storm.

Life is a classroom. There is so much wisdom to be gained from our everyday surroundings and the people around us if we just observe carefully. Don't be surprised if some of the greatest wisdom you gain comes out of the things you experience during what seems like a very ordinary day.

The wisest man is generally he who thinks himself the least so.
—NICOLAS BOILEAU-DESPREAUX

We adults have powerful influence over the young. They notice things we do that we may not even realize we are doing and absorb more about us than we think. The next thing you know, people are telling you how much your child is just like you!

How many times have you been asked, "Do you want the good news first, or the bad news?" I usually go with the bad news first because I like to end things on a positive note. However, bad news can be just a matter of your state of mind since, often, it can become good news if you look for the silver lining. It's not always easy to transform something bad into something good, but it is most rewarding when you can do it!

I often wonder what plans God has for my children. What will they do with their lives? What career path will they take? Who will they marry? Where will they live?

I asked my son, who is five years old, what he wanted to be when he grows up. I assumed he would say a policeman, fireman, or a pastor. "A daddy. That's what I want to be when I grow up!" I tried not to laugh. "That's great, honey, but what will you do for work, for your job?" "Oh," he said, "I guess I gotta find a wife."

I laughed when he said that but later realized there's probably a bit of truth in there somewhere. I remember being concerned about finding a husband—one who was the right one.

But, as we follow after God, earnestly seeking Him and His will, He takes the pressure off us.

—ASHLEY J. TAYLOR

Throughout history, a seven-day week has been a standard of many calendars. Not that people haven't tried to alter it; they have. The French revolutionaries instituted a ten-day week, but Napoleon restored the seven-day one. Russian revolutionaries turned Sunday into a working day, but Stalin restored it as a day of rest. The rhythms of our lives dictate that one day in seven is maintained as a day for us to rest. It is not important which day we choose, but our spiritual and physical health demand it. In your life, do you carve out one day to rest, or has your work spilled over into that seventh day?

All around us we see and hear echoes of humankind's spirit of proud independence. The science of an echo is truly amazing. I'm sure that as kids we all had fun shouting out something near a cave, stairwell, or cove, and were thrilled to hear the message come back to us over and over. Often, as adults, we are sent repeated messages, which we don't always respond to even the second or third time, if ever. Is there a message you have been sent more than once recently that you have been putting off replying to? It's never too late to acknowledge the call and respond.

12 MAY

The Creator is willing to do many, many things for you. Are you willing?

Are you willing . . .
To stoop down and consider the needs and
desires of little children;
to remember the weakness and loneliness of
people growing old;
to stop asking how much your friends love you,
and ask yourself if you love them enough;
to bear in mind the things that other people
have to bear in their hearts;
to try to understand what those who live
in the same home with you really want,
without waiting for them to tell you.
Are you willing to do these things even for a
day?

—ADAPTED FROM "KEEPING
CHRISTMAS," BY HENRY VAN DYKE

SHOES

Shoes divide men into three classes.
Some wear their father's shoes.
They make no declaration of their own.
Some are unthinkingly shod by the crowd.
The strong man is his own cobbler.
He insists on making his own choices.
He walks in his own shoes.

—S. D. GORDON

. . . and makes his own footprints wherever he goes!

How we respond to adversity sets the tone for how well we enjoy the good times in our lives. An understanding of how difficulty prepares us for life should alter our perspectives of how grateful we are when life seems easier. This reminds me of the well-known proverb "Don't pray for rain if you are going to complain about the mud."

The Monday-morning blues is a common affliction because Monday is the start of another workweek. However, I think we need a clearer philosophy of why we work. John Stott's story of a gardener puts some meat on the bones of this for me. As a gardener was showing a clergyman around his magnificent gardens, the clergyman was effusive in his praise to God for the miracle of creation. After a while of this, being tired of not receiving credit for his work, the gardener proclaimed, "Yeah, you should have seen this garden when God had it to himself!" If we see our jobs as the human cultivation of the responsibilities we have for our world, we can begin to see our work as a privilege and a collaboration with our Creator and other human beings.

16

MAY

At an art contest at a church bazaar, two painters entered works entitled *Peace*. The first painter's work was a scene of majestic mountains reflected in a still lake. The second painter's work was a powerful waterfall with a tree off to the side and branches drooping over the water spray. At the fork of the branch was a robin sitting in its nest. The waterfall painting won first prize, as the judges were all taken by its message of peace in the midst of potential danger.

You will keep in perfect peace him whose mind is steadfast, because he trusts in you.
—ISAIAH 26:3

It seems to me that one way or another, each of us must choose to be a slave to something. Either we choose to live life however we want, and thus become slaves to our own desires, or we choose to follow some other system of regulation and become a slave to that. If this theory is true, then our idea of freedom must be vastly different from what many of us believe it is. For me, freedom is found in obedience to that which leads to life, whereas slavery comes from obedience to that which leads to death. Which are you a slave to?

On March 20, 1980, an earthquake occurred near the summit of Mt. St. Helens, a supposedly dormant volcano in Washington, triggering avalanches. Then, on May 18, the side of Mt. St. Helens exploded, shooting tons of debris downhill at speeds of up to 150 miles per hour. The eruption lasted nine hours. Fifty-seven people lost their lives. They had been warned to leave the area but would not.

How often do we flirt with danger after we've been warned? We continue to eat unhealthy diets after our doctors have warned us about the risks. Many people still drive without wearing seatbelts despite clear evidence that doing so exponentially raises the risk of death in the case of an accident. Is there any aspect of your life in which you choose to flirt with disaster, believing it will never happen to you?

The next time I hear someone say that something is "pretty ugly," I'll take it that they really mean that it is beautiful!

"Mommy, is ugly really the new beautiful? Isn't ugly just ugly?" My son had seen a commercial for a TV show and wanted to know what the ad meant. I tried to explain that what it meant was that, even though this girl was supposedly ugly on the outside, she was a beautiful person on the inside. He wanted to know how you can see beauty on the inside—"Isn't the inside of your body all yucky?"

This was a great chance to talk about what really makes someone beautiful or attractive. It's not the makeup, wonderful haircut, or fantastic clothes. All those things will fade or go out of style, but the fruit of God's spirit in us—love, joy, peace, patience, kindness, goodness, gentleness, faithfulness, and self-control—are what will last forever. In fact, as we grow in our walk with God and reflect his character, we will only grow more beautiful as the years pass.

—Ashley J. Taylor

I am not an early riser by choice, but I have always made an effort to get my day started early so that in the evenings, when my family was all together, I could be done with the day's obligations. Starting the day on the run was a sacrifice I could not afford —without taking time to meditate and let the day unfold at its own pace, my tension and impatience hit the red zone far too frequently.

Every morning lean thine arms a while
upon the window sill of heaven—
and gaze upon thy Lord
then, with a vision in thy heart,
turn strong to meet thy day.

—THOMAS BLAKE

In his book *Good to Great,* author Jim Collins compares reaching critical mass in a company to trying to turn a giant flywheel. The effort needed to turn the wheel when it is initially still is tremendous. But once the wheel begins to move, it becomes easier and easier to turn because of the rising momentum. I think it is the same in our lives. When things just don't seem to be working out for me, I am sometimes suspicious that it is because I am just waiting for something to happen. Instead, if I get up and move—use the gifts God gave me to improve my circumstances as best I can—then I tend to see things, often unrelated things, begin to happen.

Providence sends food for the birds but does not throw it in the nest.
—MARION ARTHUR

Some proverbs are so short they seem as though they'd be easy to keep in mind, but I have so much trouble remembering them, I must always remind myself by reading them over. I may not always remember each phrase, and so often I can't measure up to the ideas, but I'd hate to think what kind of person I'd be if I didn't at least try to live them as best I can.

Today we have cell phones that can chime, calculate, wake us up, send e-mails, show photos, and even talk. Yet people are still late for meetings and other events. Instead of asking technology to help us be more responsible, are we asking it to be responsible *for* us?

There is a time for everything, and a season for every activity under heaven.
—ECCLESIASTES 3:1

Vernon Grounds tells a wonderful story that helps me immensely in times of discouragement:

A college student decided one summer that he would earn money for his tuition by selling Bibles door to door. He began at the home of the school president. The president's wife came to the door and explained politely that her family didn't need any more books. As the student walked away, she saw him limping. "Oh, I'm sorry," she exclaimed. "I didn't know you were disabled!"

When the student turned around, she realized she had offended him. So she quickly added, "I didn't mean anything except admiration. But doesn't your disability color your life?" To which the student responded, "Yes, it does. But thank God, I can choose the color."

How selflessly do you love your friends, spouse, and children? You might die for them, but would you change the radio station for them?

Today is ours: why do we fear?
Today is ours: we have it here;
Let's banish business, banish sorrow:
To the future belongs tomorrow.
—ADAPTED FROM "THE EPICURE,"
BY ABRAHAM COWLEY

How many times has someone barked at you to do something that needed to be done, but never lifted a finger to help? It is said that "others will follow your footsteps more easily than they will follow your advice."

It's true that women have done zillions of amazing things and anyone of us has the potential to do just about anything. If there is something that you have been thinking of doing but have been putting off because you are unsure of yourself, now is the time to take action and make it happen. Don't worry about the final outcome; just take one step toward your goal, then another and another. You may accomplish something even greater than you ever thought you were capable of.

They talk about a woman's sphere,
as though it had a limit;
there's not a place in earth or heaven,
there's not a task to mankind given,
there's not a blessing or a woe,
there's not a whisper, yes or no,
there's not a life, or death, or birth,
that has a feather's weight of worth,
without a woman in it.

—KATE FIELD

Every child born into this world is a new thought of God, an ever fresh and radiant possibility.

—KATE DOUGLAS WIGGIN

There are no endings, only new beginnings.

—FLAVIA

*A reporter in our local newspaper was
writing about an interview with an elderly
gentleman on his 99th birthday. After the
interview, the reporter mentioned that he
hoped to see the man on his 100th birthday,
to which the older gentleman replied, "I don't
see why not. You look healthy enough to me!"*
—REVEREND LEROY GAGER

While in a church in Glasgow, we were told a story of David Livingstone. When God asked him, "What is that in thine hand?" David answered, "My heart—for Africa," and accepted God's challenge to missionary service.

We often look at our hands and think there's nothing we can give with them. God doesn't look at our hands like we do. He is more interested in our availability than our ability.

If you are too busy to pray for your children, you are too busy.

The most difficult thing for a mother to remember is that other people have perfect children too. There is only one perfect child in the world and every mother has it.

—CHINESE PROVERB

31

M
A
Y

June has two birthstones. Often set in white or yellow gold, the pearl is valued according to its color, shape, and size. June's other gem, the moonstone, has a soft sheen and is translucent, with shades of white, pink, yellow, and blue. The main flower of the month is the rose; another is the honeysuckle. Both come in various colors and represent friendship, love, happiness, strength, and beauty.

JUNE

Through the footprints of faith, we see everything that God is. To really get the most out of life, we have to take things one step at a time and enjoy each moment.

Television is the way it is because we continue to watch it. We have more channels and more selection than ever before, but do we have more quality? It's so easy to keep on watching something that really isn't very good.

Be selective. Even better, turn off your TV and turn on your mind.

Do you ever have a day when you just don't know which way is up? On these days, I think to myself, "Why am I being persecuted like this; am I being strengthened by this experience for some reason unknown to me?" As children, we all fall and scrape our knees, and at the time it seems like a tragedy. But we all soon learn to be more careful, which in turn protects us from something that could be much worse.

At the close of his will, American statesman Patrick Henry stated,

"This is all the inheritance I give to my dear family. The religion of Christ will give them one which will make them rich indeed."

It's often when there's a death in the family that we ponder the meaning of life the most. What means the most in life is what we put into it. That's right, we determine what—and how much—we put into our lives and those of the people around us. The meaning of life, therefore, is what we decide to make it.

The next time you engage in an argument, first make sure that you clearly comprehend the other person's point of view. Many times, you will find that you misunderstood it, and once clarified, there is no longer anything to argue about.

Misunderstanding is the source of untold sorrows.

—PAUL L. POWERS

It is love that makes a home. The property may be old, the furnishings worn, but if love fills the house it is a palace. Thank God I live in a palace.

—PAUL L. POWERS

Love is not in our choice, but in our fate.
—JOHN DRYDEN

Robert Frost probably said it a little more
clearly: "Love is an irresistible desire to be
irresistibly desired." Are you irresistible?

Wherever you go and whatever you do, don't forget to take the most important thing with you: your smile. It won't cost you anything, and you may even get one in return.

There are all sorts of energy drinks available now and some are even more addictive than coffee. However, many of us have gotten used to drinking them to jolt ourselves out of the state we are in, waking ourselves up to meet the reality of the day. I recently heard that coffee and some energy drinks actually require more energy for our bodies to break down and process than we get from the beverage itself. I guess that explains the "flatness" we sometimes feel an hour or so after consuming these drinks. There's nothing better than eight hours' sleep and time spent in daily prayer to keep us alert and engaged with life.

Life can be so dull sometimes. I get so overwhelmed by the mundane that I stop noticing the beauty around me. I crawl in my daily footsteps with God. I view my family as a job instead of a blessing. I get lazy living in a wealthy, lethargic land and take for granted my relationships with both God and with my family. I enjoy my comfort zone. I enjoy my space. Then suddenly I'm jolted right out of it!

—P. M. CALLAHAN

Have you ever found yourself in a meeting where there is a great buzz and ideas are really flowing? Then a day or two or even a week later, you find that no one has actually done anything that was recommended. Well, maybe this would be a great opportunity for you to take on a leadership role to at least start the ball rolling. Who knows, it could lead to a promotion or other rewarding opportunity. Either way, people will take note and see you as a doer.

The world is divided into people who do things and people who get the credit.
—DWIGHT MORROW

Try, if you can, to belong to the first class. There's far less competition.

An example of faith is discovering that you have left a set of footprints where you didn't expect to leave them.

STEP BY STEP

He does not lead me year by year
Nor even day by day,
But step by step my path unfolds,
My Lord directs my way.
Tomorrow's plans I do not know
I only know this minute!
But He will say, "This is the way,
By faith now walk ye in it."
—BARBARA C. RYBERG

11

JUNE

It's pretty challenging sometimes to see the future in both a long-term and a short-term way at the same time. Maybe that's why they invented bifocals!

*Many people
seem to be worried about
the end of the world.
Other people
are only worried about
the end of the month.*

—HEATHER KAITLYN BARCLAY

It's so much better to be remembered for doing something good than to be remembered for forgetting to do it!

Two newly married men were discussing their goals and ambitions in an outdoor café. One man said, "I just want to do something that will be remembered for a long time and talked about constantly." The other man replied, "That's easy—just forget your wife's birthday!"

—PAUL L. POWERS

When I feel I've overextended myself and regret making promises that I am not able to keep, this old saying sometimes helps keeps me going: "After all is said and done, more is usually said than done."

It's so easy to say yes to requests, so much easier than saying no, especially to those who are closest to us. However, you will always be further ahead if you promise only the things you know you can deliver.

TREASURES OF THE HEART

Rich treasures in the gold mine of life
we're called to dig up ourselves.
It seems a miner faces strife
as lethargy each man fells.

Rich nuggets of gold and silver
now hold no attraction for me,
and diamond, garnet, and sapphire
are not the treasures I see.

Rich treasure in the gold mine of life
is the gemstone called "a soul,"
cut by trials as sharp as a knife.
God help me see past the coal.

—MFP

Consider the saying below, which asks for the best from us.

There are two good rules which ought to be written on every heart—never to believe anything bad about anybody unless you positively know it to be true; never to tell even that unless you feel that it is absolutely necessary, and that God is listening.

—HENRY VAN DYKE

W e sometimes mistakenly believe that money is the most important thing for successfully raising a family. Don't get me wrong—I know that it costs a lot to raise a family these days. But the lack of a loving spirit, or of communication and compromise, has ruined more family relationships than a lack of money.

A father is a fellow who has replaced the currency in his wallet with snapshots of his kids.

—AUTHOR UNKNOWN

17

JUNE

The sooner you realize that you don't know it all, the smarter you will be.

By the time a man realizes that maybe his father was right, he usually has a son who thinks he's wrong.

—CHARLES WADSWORTH

Take time to honestly reflect on what you have done, as your past can often reveal what your future holds.

A FATHER'S MIRROR

What do you see in the mirror?
I asked my reflection there.
I see a face that is weary and worn
and a brow with receding hair.
So now there's no reflection there.
I smashed the mirror in anger,
To reveal the truth in me.

—M. M. SIMPSON

When I am tempted to ignore the advice of those around me in favor of my own ideas, I like to reflect on an old Native American proverb: "Listen, or your tongue will keep you deaf."

Listen, my son, to your father's instruction, and do not forsake your mother's teaching.
—PROVERBS 1:8

My grandson came home from his second day in grade one. His father asked him how he liked his new teacher. "Oh," Calvin replied, "she's not so smart. She's always asking us questions because she doesn't know the answers to the problems."

A long time ago I realized my life will never be free of problems. Soon after that I realized that most of our best opportunities in life are wonderfully disguised as roadblocks that take us in a different direction from what we intended.

I have a friend who is sometimes afraid to try new things. At those times, I like to quote these anonymous words: "Never be afraid to try something new. Remember, amateurs built the ark. Professionals built the *Titanic*."

There was a young lady named Kinter,
who married a man in the winter.
The man's name was Wood,
and now, as they should,
the Woods have a cute little "splinter."

—AUTHOR UNKNOWN

When you doubt yourself and worry you are not good enough for the task at hand, think about nature and how wonderful it is because of its diversity. It would be really depressing if the only birdsongs we heard came from the three most prominent birds.

Since we've been married, my husband moves with his job about every three years like clockwork! We find a church in the new city, get a house, get settled. We're thinking this time we'll stay at least ten years, maybe twenty years, and I start feeling cozy. Then God calls us somewhere else, and I start packing boxes again. I'm reminded of the story of Ruth—"whither thou goest I will go."
—P. M. CALLAHAN

Furnishings for your heavenly home have all been sent on ahead.

Don't waste time looking for happiness outside of yourself. True happiness can come only from within.

I admire those of today's younger generations who don't seem as tempted as my generation was to take their identity from what they do for a living. I have seen too many seniors struggle with retirement because their whole lives were wrapped up in their careers. So remember, it is not what you do that makes you who you are but, rather, what you have left behind that will encourage the next generation on to greater things.

Works without faith are like a fish without water, it wants the element it should live in. A building without a basis cannot stand; faith is the foundation, and every good action is as a stone laid.

—OWEN FELTHAM

If the two of you truly become one, under the umbrella of marriage, you will be so much stronger and more effective in everything you do together.

The marriage certificate is not a certificate of ownership but, rather, one of partnership.
—PAUL L. POWERS

My husband, a longtime admirer of the eagle, has collected photos and artwork of the bird over the years. His most amazing oil painting is one in which the eagle's eyes seem to look at you no matter where you are in the room. The artist must have spent a great deal of time getting to know his subject.

The eagle that soars near the sun is not concerned how it will cross the raging stream.
—AUTHOR UNKNOWN

I wish not worrying were as simple as telling myself not to worry. I know I cannot change things by worrying. I know worrying exhausts me more than the hardest work. The best way I've ever found to keep myself from worrying is to do something good for another person—to get my thoughts off my own situation. Come to think of it, that usually puts most of my problems in perspective!

Enjoy the little things. One day you might find they weren't so little after all.

The smallest act of kindness is worth more than the grandest intention.

—OSCAR WILDE

Alice Lucie Kinnear, who turned ninety-one in October 2007, shared with our family an interesting *Titanic* story that she had carried in her heart from childhood.

As a young Salvation Army officer squeezed in at the side of a lifeboat to make room for others to climb aboard, his hand dragged heavily over the boat's edge into the cold water. But instead of water, his fingers touched fabric. He immediately turned and pulled into his lap a bundle of tartan containing a blue-faced baby. Quickly, he tucked the tiny infant under his heavy coat and inside his shirt, praying for the mercy of God on every soul still on board the sinking ship.

In the early morning stream of light, the *Carpathia* gradually rescued seventeen lifeboats, including the one containing the young officer. Aboard the ship and still cradling the hidden child, he saw a woman weeping helplessly. He comforted others as he cautiously made his way to her side. "Take heart, God has saved you," he said. But she was inconsolable. "You don't understand! I dropped my baby when I got into the lifeboat. *She's lost! She's lost!*" the woman wailed. Elated, the young officer reached under his shirt to present a now warm, pink, and sleeping little baby girl. Who could know the joy of a grieving mother, believing her child dead but having her returned . . . and in fine health despite her ordeal? This was all because God placed a willing hand in the icy wave.

The birthstone for July is the ruby. July has several flowers associated with it, including the water lily and larkspur. The larkspur is a symbol of lightness and an open heart, while the water lily is associated with eloquence, persuasion, and purity of heart.

JULY

"There was only one set of footprints. I realized that this was at the lowest and saddest times of my life."

Have you ever noticed that no matter how big your family is, or how many friends you have, when you go through a bad time you always feel alone? It's like this for everyone. And so in "Footprints," I use this realization at the heart of the piece to touch on a universal truth—that when we feel lost and alone, God is always with us, silent though he may sometimes be.

Those who have been captivated by the love of gardening often find—as Mary Sarton once said—that the hobby is an instrument of grace. The practice of tending a living thing is a reminder of how resilient life is. No matter how many mistakes we make with our own plantings, all around us we see that life flourishes even in the most difficult places and adverse circumstances. Despite our own challenges, we can flourish, too.

Every flower is a soul blossoming in nature.
—GERARD DE NERVAL

Life has a funny way of sometimes leading us down the paths we least want to go. But regardless of where you are today, it is still possible to gain wisdom from the world around you and to grow, come the rain, the dew, the darkness, and the light.

We must endure the valleys to enjoy the mountains. And when we descend into the valleys, it is our memories of the mountains that drive us to strive for them again.

They ask not your planting,
they need not your care
as they grow.
Dropped down in the valley,
the field, anywhere,
there they grow;
They grow in their beauty,
arrayed in pure white;
they grow,
Clothed in glory,
by heaven's own light
sweetly grow.
The grasses are clothed
and the ravens are fed
from his store;
But you,
who are guarded and led,
how much more,
Will he clothe you,
and feed you,
and give you his care.
Then leave it with him;
he has, everywhere,
ample store.

—MFP

So much of life is about balance. We should watch what we eat but not focus on it so much that our self-esteem is tied to everything we put in our mouths.

You don't have to be a teacher to teach. We all have something that we can share with others; but when doing so, share your knowledge with humility and not pride—the lesson will sink in much deeper.

No one intentionally grows weeds. But sometimes less experienced gardeners will plant a seed that grows to be something other than what they expected. Perhaps it turns out to be less colorful; maybe it doesn't grow at all. But the studious gardener will read the descriptions of plants and try to understand exactly what he or she has planted.

Like the studious gardener, we should keep in mind that many of our short-term decisions turn into long-term consequences. When we make decisions carelessly, we have to be prepared for less-than-desirable results.

Our responses to many of life's trials seem to boil down to just a couple of options—fight or give up. And there are actually very few times when you should give up.

THE MAN WHO THINKS HE CAN
If you think you are beaten, you are.
If you think you dare not, you don't.
If you'd like to win, but think you can't,
It's almost a cinch you won't.
If you think you'll lose, you're lost.
For out in the world we find
Success begins with a fellow's will;
it's all in the state of mind.

—MFP

One thing I admire about young adults today is that their approach to work is often healthier than the approach of previous generations. I am proud to be from a country known for its hard workers, but I am more proud to know that our hard workers today are not sacrificing eternal things like home and family in exchange for the fleeting success of business.

Think about the place you call home. Is it somewhere you want to come home to? If not, what can you do to make it more of a sanctuary?

A fugitive is one who is running from home. A vagabond is one who has no home. A stranger is one away from home. A pilgrim is one on his way home.

—AUTHOR UNKNOWN

12

JULY

People usually go on vacation to forget, and when they open their luggage they learn what it was they forgot.

—AUTHOR UNKNOWN

If you are fortunate enough to have had friends for many years, send them a note telling them how thankful you are for their loyalty through all the ins and outs of your life.

THAT SPECIAL GIFT

There is no more human quality for me
than the jewel of abiding loyalty,
for when crafty fair-weather friends stray
    away
the one who remains loyal sustains my day.
                                    —AUTHOR UNKNOWN

Most things in life, when you give them away, leave you poorer—things like money and objects. But some things you give away become assets, returning many times over the amount you give. These include grace, hope, and love.

It's often been said that listening is
a tremendous stimulant. It's hard enough
to truly listen to others, but how often
do we simply listen to our own thoughts?
Here's an experiment to try: Next time you
are tempted to turn on the radio—whether
in the car or elsewhere—instead let
yourself exist in the silence and listen to
your own thoughts. I find that we already
hold the answers to many of our questions,
and we'd discover them if we'd just take the
time to listen to our hearts.

One ear it heard, at the other, out it went.
—Geoffrey Chaucer

A woman is like a teabag. You never know how strong she is until she gets into hot water.
—ELEANOR ROOSEVELT

We all need to take a moment now and then to recognize our personal strengths and pour them out on those who need our assistance, whether you're in hot water or not.

A friend is someone who, when you have been apart for a long time, can simply continue the conversations you've had for years without bothering to assess how you've changed in the meantime.

The relations of Christians to each other are like the several flowers in a garden that have upon each the dew of heaven, which, being shaken by the wind, they let all the dew at each other's roots, whereby they are jointly nourished, and become nourishers of one another.

—JOHN BUNYAN

In her book *Further Thoughts on Faith,* Anne Lamott gives a wonderful idea for hosting what she calls a stay-at-home cruise. For a single day, she spoils herself without leaving home, focusing on the act of refreshing her body and spirit without succumbing to the demands of the television, telephone, or calendar. How can you spoil yourself today without leaving home?

In his book *Emotions Revealed,* Paul Ekman tells of his work studying the facial expressions of people around the world and discusses how our expressions are the same because of the human condition, not because of our culture. In an effort to catalog many of the revealing expressions of people around the world, Ekman and his partner photographed themselves displaying numerous emotions. A sidebar finding to their work was that regardless of how they actually felt, when they spent time forcing their faces into poses of grief and sadness, their emotions followed suit. Likewise, displaying the pleasant emotions always made them happy. Try it today—see if you can intentionally make yourself feel better simply by smiling.

Love the truth, but be forgiving of errors.

Love means to commit oneself without guarantee, to give oneself completely in the hope that our love will produce love in the loved person. Love is an act of faith, and whoever is of little faith is also of little love.
—ERICH FROMM

Laugh and the world laughs with you. Weep and you weep alone.
—ELLA WHEELER WILCOX

Or at the very least, try smiling. No matter what language you speak, a smile will always be understood.

True friends are like so many other important things in our lives—we take them for granted until they are gone and we realize what we have lost.

I wondered, should I speak to her?
She was sitting all alone,
at a table that was close to mine,
where I sat on my own;
"Well," I ventured with a smile,
"Isn't it fine weather?"
And before our coffees had gone cold,
two strangers sat together.

—PHYLLIS ELLISON

You just can't please everyone. Sometimes we bend over backwards trying to help others, many times at the expense of ourselves or those who really deserve our assistance. Weigh carefully who you help and who you can show how to help, so that they can help others, too.

Isn't it amazing that when we go swimming in the ocean, any cuts or scrapes we have heal up so fast? The same is true when we gargle with salt water to soothe a sore throat. Everything in nature has a purpose and benefit, if used in the right measure.

Love is the salt of life; a higher taste, it gives to pleasure, and then makes it last.
—JOHN SHEFFIELD,
FIRST DUKE OF BUCKINGHAM

Looking back can slow us down.
Looking ahead keeps us heaven bound.

One day at a time—
this is enough.
Do not look back
and grieve over the past,
for it is gone,
and do not be troubled
about the future,
for it has not yet come.
Live in the present,
and make it so beautiful
that it will be worth
remembering.

—IDA SCOTT TAYLOR

I received this little ditty from a woman in Florida and thought I would pass it on:

*Hey diddle, diddle, I've a bulge in my middle,
and I'm working to whittle it soon.
But eating's such fun I can't get it done,
Till my dish runs away with my spoon!*

For most of human history, people have been nourishing their bodies without the aid of nutritional science. Granted, sometimes life ended badly at a young age. In the twenty-first century, it seems that the principles of nutritional science change every few years or so. But no matter what revisions are made, a healthy lifestyle always includes these two fundamentals: exercise and eating our veggies.

When you give all of your love at the altar, never *alter* how you give all of your love ever after.

With this ring I thee wed, with my body I thee worship, and with all my worldly goods I thee endow.
                    —*Book of Common Prayer*

I heard it as a young married person, and have seen it borne out over and over again—the best thing a man can do for his children is to love their mother.

A successful marriage requires falling in love many times over, and always with the same person.

—GERMAINE GREER

Love is so nonrational it is hard to understand how it is the cure to the world's ills. But few would disagree that it is so.

To love someone deeply gives you strength. Being loved by someone deeply gives you courage.

—LAO TZU

Computer technology is evolving so fast that I can hardly keep up. Over the course of writing this book, I lost an important attachment and had to rewrite some of the lost material. Computers make *very* fast, *very* accurate mistakes. They tend to send my best material to cyberspace. However, I can always be sure that when I "download" a prayer or "upload" praise to the Almighty, it will never get lost in the Ethernet.

In a winning relationship, one plus one equals won.

He is the half part of a blessed man
left to be finished by such as she:
and she a fair divided excellence
whose fullness of perfection lies in him.
                              —WILLIAM SHAKESPEARE,
                              King John

Every birthstone has its own relative value, holding a special meaning in the month it represents. Peridot, the gemstone for August, comes in shades of green, brown, and olive, and symbolizes love, truth, faithfulness, and loyalty. The gladiolus and the poppy, which represent beauty, strength of character, love, marriage, and family, are the flowers associated with this month.

AUGUST

God is not afraid of our questions. This basic understanding supports the poem "Footprints." When things do not go well, we want and expect someone to provide solutions to our problems. Of course, the bad situations we occasionally face don't always happen for any particular reason. And although we don't always get the answers that we hope to get from God, we can rest assured that we have no secrets from him. And if I have no secrets, I might as well challenge him with questions about what I don't appreciate in life.

Don't get caught fooling yourself or, even worse, others. No one can know something about everything, and deep wisdom comes only from learning and years of experience. So never be afraid to learn something from anyone, as even the underprivileged, the uneducated, and the young have experiences that we can learn from.

The greatest of fools is he who imposes on himself, and in his greatest concern thinks certainly he knows that which he has least studied, and of which he is profoundly ignorant.

—EARL OF SHAFTESBURY

None but a fool is always right.

—DAVID HARE

It's so true that you never get a second chance to make a good first impression. Within the first few seconds, people pass judgment on you, and once the first impression is made, it's virtually irreversible. How fortunate we are that when our final judgment day comes, the Almighty will not dismiss us by the things that we first did.

Many times while I was growing up, I would sit on a stool and watch my mother roll dough for bread, cinnamon rolls, or some kind of pie. It was fascinating to see how long it took to roll . . . and reroll until the dough was just perfect.

Love doesn't just sit there like a stone; it has to be made like bread, remade all the time, made new.

—URSULA K. LE GUIN

Instill in children a sense of purpose. Young people today are saturated by materialism more than ever before. Unfortunately, material objects don't bring lasting joy. Teach your children how to look for something they can do to make the world a better place. Help them to see that even though they are children, they have their whole lives ahead of them to accomplish many good things. If they get started now thinking about what they can achieve, then who knows what they may be able to accomplish.

Our children will surprise us with great delight, if we inspire them.

Each year at our annual costume party for All Hallows' Eve, we enjoy a game that gets the entire party laughing. Everybody gets the opportunity to whisper a little message to the person next to him or her. That person in turn repeats the message to the next one, and on around the circle it goes. By the time the whispered message gets around the room, it is completely different from the original, and everyone has a hearty laugh.

This game is a good reminder to me to state my criticisms—and especially my praises—in a very clear, calm, and unhurried way so that there is little chance that my words will be misunderstood.

The saying goes "Values are not taught; they're caught."

Have you ever thought of yourself as a mentor? It's a great challenge for us as adults to always set a good example and be solid role models for young people. You can be sure that kids will be quick to remind you of things *you've* done at just the moment you tell them not to do something *you* think is wrong. Setting a good example means leaving footprints behind that you would be proud to have anyone follow in.

Have you ever noticed how everyone else's vacation tales make for the most boring stories but yours are fabulously interesting?

The speediest days in all creation,
must surely be those in a two-week vacation.
—ASHLEY J. TAYLOR

How come politicians today never talk like this?

You cannot bring about prosperity by discouraging thrift.

You cannot strengthen the weak by weakening the strong.

You cannot help small men by tearing down big men.

You cannot help the poor by destroying the rich.

You cannot lift the wage-earner by pulling down the wage-payer.

You cannot keep out of trouble by spending more than your income.

You cannot further the brotherhood of man by inciting class hatred.

You cannot establish sound security on borrowed money.

You cannot build character and courage by taking away a man's initiative and independence.

You cannot help men permanently by doing for them what they could and should do for themselves.

—REVEREND WILLIAM JOHN HENRY BOETCKER

Learn to smile when life's got you down. It's a chance to prove your strength.

Too many people pray for emergency rations rather than daily bread.

—PAUL L. POWERS

Most people miss opportunities because they look so much like work.

For yesterday
is but a dream
and tomorrow
is only a vision
but today
well lived
makes yesterday
a dream of happiness
and every tomorrow
a vision of hope.

—SANSKRIT PROVERB

11

AUGUST

I inherited my mother's tailoring scissors and had them in the bottom of my knitting and crocheting bag as I boarded a plane on September 10, 2001. The luggage inspector just thought they were rather enormous scissors and put them back in my bag. Needless to say, the world changed the next day, and I never carried them again. The thought of how air travel has changed forever reminds me to appreciate what I have, down to the smallest things I take for granted.

13

AUGUST

Who really cares
if the wind doesn't blow,
if the sun doesn't shine,
if the grass doesn't grow?

Who really cares
about the man on the street
with no shoes on his feet,
with no shelter or food to eat?

Who really cares
if you live or die,
if you laugh or cry,
tell the truth or a lie?

Who really cares?
Well, God really cares.
Do you know he loves you?
Do you love him too?

—MFP

It has always struck me that the men with the biggest inferiority complexes are those who drive cars that are too big and those who are intimidated by smart women.

SUCCESS

He has achieved success
who has lived well, laughed often, and loved
much;
who has enjoyed the trust of pure women, the
respect of intelligent men and the love of
little children;
who has filled his niche and accomplished his
task;
who has never lacked appreciation of Earth's
beauty or failed to express it;
who has left the world better than he found it,
whether an improved poppy, a perfect poem,
or a rescued soul;
who has always looked for the best in others
and given them the best he had;
whose life was an inspiration;
whose memory a benediction.
—BESSIE ANDERSON STANLEY

I just brought out my bathing suit to go for a refreshing swim, but I kind of feel like putting it away. It always seems that when we put on our bathing suits, we wish that we had started dieting and exercising earlier.

Did you ever wonder if there was any relationship between the number of cookbooks and the number of diet books that are available today? The diet that has always worked the best for me is the "eat less diet." And you don't need a book to tell you how to go about it!

Dr. Billy Graham said that if he were to live life over again he would schedule "family time" just as surely as anything else. One's family should always be a main source of happiness—second only to God. Make sure your family ties are tight!

Most girls seem to marry men like their fathers. Maybe that's the reason so many mothers cry at weddings.

—AUTHOR UNKNOWN

Castles in the air are great until you step out the door.

It was always great fun to build sandcastles at the beach in White Rock, BC, at the sandcastle competition, but equally sad to return the following morning and find the beach flat as far as the eye could see. There would not be even the slightest clue that the previous day had been a special day of sandcastles.

Castles in the air, or on the beach, are temporary, just like everything we possess here on earth.

Faith is easy when life is good but can be difficult when it's not. It's easy to believe a rope is strong when you are just tying up a box with it, but when you are hanging from a cliff by that same rope, you find out how much faith you really have.

The shuttles of His purpose move
To carry out His own design;
Seek not too soon to disapprove
His work, nor yet assign
Dark motives, when, with silent tread,
You view some sombre fold;
For lo, within each darker thread
There twines a thread of gold.

Spin cheerfully,
Not tearfully,
He knows the way you plod;
Spin carefully,
Spin prayerfully,
But leave the thread with God.

—MFP

Gardening is an opportunity
to experiment with life without hurting
anyone.

*Flowers are the sweetest things God ever made
and forgot to put a soul into.*
—Henry Ward Beecher

Each fall we travel to Great Britain and other countries in Europe to visit people in hospitals, schools, churches, prisons, and nursing homes, as well as to reach out on the radio and television. A few years ago, I asked our driver about the meaning of a street sign that said "Changed priorities ahead." He answered, "It has to do with how we give way to the traffic in our roundabout. We yield to a different driver than usual."

Sometimes God places this sign in our lives—"Changed priorities ahead"—and we need to hear his call and follow him. This can make it so much easier to negotiate the busy road ahead and to make it smoother for other drivers on that same road.

I can't say it any better than this familiar line: "Life, like a mirror, never gives back more than we put into it."

THE MIRROR

One day a rich man of a miserly disposition visited a rabbi, who took him by the hand and led him to a window. "Look out there," said the rabbi. The rich man looked out into the street. "What do you see?"

"I see men and women and children."

Again the rabbi took him by the hand, but this time led him to a mirror. "What do you see now?"

"I see myself."

Then the rabbi said, "Behold, the window there is glass, and the mirror is glass also. But the glass of the mirror is covered with silver. No sooner is silver added than you cease to see others and see only yourself."

—OLIVER WENDELL HOLMES

Don't hesitate, go and see that friend or acquaintance who needs a helping hand. We can't do everything that needs to be done, or help everyone who needs help, but there's nothing worse than looking back on your life with disappointment over the things you wish you had done.

Footprints in the sands of time never can be made by sitting down.

—AUTHOR UNKNOWN

The wonderful thing about doing a good turn for someone is that you sometimes unexpectedly get one back in re*turn*.

He who receives a benefit should never forget it; he who bestows should never remember it.
—Pierre Charron

GIVE

*Give, though your gift be small, still be a
     giver;*
out of the little fount proceeds the river;
out of the river's gifts gulfs soon will be
pouring their waters out, making a sea.
*Out of the sea again Heaven draws its
     showers,*
and to the fount imparts all its new powers.
Thus in the circle born, gifts roll around,
and in the blessings given,
blessing is found.

—AUTHOR UNKNOWN

*Accept who you are. Without that, you will
never feel as though you are good enough or
deserving enough to succeed.*

—PAUL L. POWERS

The world is more interested in what you practice than in what you profess. No matter how often you say something, it is not until you do it that it makes a difference to others.

No talent, no self-denial, no brains, no character, is required to set up in the grumbling business; but those who are moved by a genuine desire to do good have little time for murmuring or complaint.

—ROBERT WEST

Some people grumble all of the time; it's something that we do mostly out of habit. But what if we were to try to find two good things to say first, before cranking out a grumble? I bet that the grumbling business would soon be put out of business.

How well do we know our neighbors? We give them a friendly nod or wave, or a "Hi, how are you?" But do we really know if they are lonely and need someone to talk to over a cup of tea? "Loving your neighbor as yourself" goes well beyond a friendly nod or wave.

Once while in China I asked a local man what it meant to be Chinese. After thinking a moment, he replied that it meant living with family in a beautiful country. As I thought about how the culture of the Western world values independence and mobility, I wondered what it would be like to live in a world where those two sets of values are considered equal.

As a teacher, I often found myself learning some of the most interesting things from my students. What is really rewarding is presenting students with something that you don't know the answer to yourself, and working out the answer together. I was the most satisfied and happy when my students went on to learn so much more than I could ever teach them.

There is this difference between happiness and wisdom that he who thinks himself the happiest man really is so; but he who thinks himself the wisest, is generally the greatest fool.
—CHARLES CALEB COLTON

There is no shame in failing at something, only in not trying in the first place.

It's good to keep in mind that the learning process would be much more difficult if we never made mistakes or failed at anything. So don't be afraid to take on new challenges or try to do something that you haven't tried before. At the very least you will know what you can't do, but many times you will find something that you can do!

Discipline comes from the ability to say no to ourselves.

If someone puts out a bowl of nuts or opens up a bag of chips, you know that you can't just stop at a handful. Discipline comes from the ability to say no to ourselves. If we don't, then others may end up saying no for us.

The birthstone for September is the sapphire, which reminds us of love and wisdom. The flower for this month is the aster. It comes in pink and purple, and represents devotion, daintiness, and light.

SEPTEMBER

Perhaps the most obvious thing about "Footprints" is something that I find I have to keep reminding myself of: God promises to be with us all the time, but he never promises that things will be easy.

In the hope of bigger and better things, we often miss the flowers that have been at our feet all summer.

By all these lovely tokens
September days are here,
with summer's best of weather
and autumn's best of cheer.
                    —HELEN HUNT JACKSON

If you desire to know what people are like without all the pretense and politics of life, just look at a child.

Unless we reach our children's hearts today, they will break our hearts tomorrow.
—MOTTO OF LITTLE PEOPLE'S
MINISTRY ASSOCIATION OF CANADA

3 SEPTEMBER

There is nothing we can ever do for our kids that is wasted effort. They seldom say "thanks" or pat us on the back for our work. But what we invest in them is absorbed like water on a hot day.

Nobody knows what a boy is worth, and the world must wait and see. But for every man in an honored place a boy once used to be.

—AUTHOR UNKNOWN

Religion has been studied and practiced for ages, but it has been studied far more than it has been practiced.

—AUTHOR UNKNOWN

When it comes to religious teachings and history, there is so much to study that it could take a lifetime to absorb most of what there is to know. Fortunately, though, it takes only a few moments to put many of the basic principles into practice.

—PAUL L. POWERS

Both giving and receiving criticism that is truly objective are two of life's greatest skills.

Don't mind criticism: if it's untrue, disregard it; if it's unfair, keep yourself from irritation; if it's ignorant, smile; if it's justified, learn from it.

—E. C. McKenzie

H

ave you ever wondered why you were made the way you are or how you ended up living where you do? The almighty Creator has designed our world and our lives right down to the most minute detail, with specific purposes in mind.

8 SEPTEMBER

School days can be the happiest days of your life—if your kids are old enough to attend.

Do not handicap your children by making their lives easy.

—ROBERT A. HEINLEIN

How fortunate would we be if fear of failure never stood in anyone's way?

Don't be afraid to take a big step if one is indicated; you can't cross a chasm in two small jumps.

—David Lloyd George

9 SEPTEMBER

When I begin to cut myself off from the world—staying indoors because going out is too much trouble—reflecting on this quote humbles me and reminds me to never take nature for granted.

The best remedy for those who are afraid, lonely, or unhappy is to go outside, somewhere where they can be quiet, alone with the heavens, nature, and God. Because only then does one feel that all is as it should be.
—ANNE FRANK

The World Trade Center's twin towers collapsed on September 11, 2001, after two planes struck them. The air attacks killed nearly 3,000 people. This day will long be remembered and grieved over by people around the world.

Health, happiness, and success depend upon the fighting spirit of each person. The big thing is not what happens to us in life but what we do about what happens to us.
—GEORGE ALLEN

11

SEPTEMBER

Our lives often feel most full of purpose when we are setting out on a significant challenge.

Set your goals high enough to inspire you and low enough to encourage you.

—AUTHOR UNKNOWN

Asign on the front door of a roadside restaurant read:

So you like homemade bread?
So you like homemade biscuits?
So you like homemade pies?
THEN GO HOME!

Whenever someone makes a dessert from scratch, the notion of "the good old days" comes up. And when it does, I silently wonder, "Were those also the good old days when people had to beat their laundry against rocks and make their own soap? Because if they are one and the same, bring on the boxed goodies!"

13

SEPTEMBER

14

SEPTEMBER

How you begin is not nearly as important as how you finish.

Some people are like blotters—they soak up everything but get it backwards.

—AUTHOR UNKNOWN

We are all prisoners of our own experiences. To escape a painful past means believing it doesn't dictate your future.

Failing is life's way of teaching us how to handle success. Victory without struggle is meaningless. After all, if we didn't have any struggles or failures, we would never genuinely know the meaning and joy of success.

Why is it that some friends drop out of our lives as though they were never there? Has this happened to you? Has it happened more than once recently? If so, is it because of something you have done or are doing? Take a moment to reflect and honestly search for the reason this may have happened. Maybe it's time to call this person and invite him or her out for a cup of coffee.

18

SEPTEMBER

If you heard a bit of gossip, whether false or
*   whether true,*
Be it of a friend or stranger, let me tell you
*   what to do.*
Button your lips securely lest the tale you
*   should repeat*
Would bring sorrow unto someone whose life
*   now is very sweet.*

—MFP

Years ago, I used to get upset with my parents for spoiling my children. Then I realized that if they didn't, maybe no one would. Sometimes I think that my childhood was much more difficult than my children's. I guess my parents must have felt the same way about their childhoods.

20

SEPTEMBER

The most sincere people will make enough mistakes to make them humble. Thank God for mistakes and take courage. Don't give up on account of them.

—PAUL L. POWERS

If you try to find greatness or think you have achieved it, that's exactly when you may be in for a big surprise. There is a difference between doing a great job and doing a job that is great. Ask yourself this: Did you do a great job, or is it the job itself that has made you great? Greatness will find you; there's no need to look for it.

I was down on my knees scrubbing a black mark off the kitchen floor with water from the rain bucket. Our next door neighbor's four-year-old stood in the hallway and watched. Finally, she said, "Miss M., are you wearing those yellow rubber gloves so your hands don't wrinkle more and get so rusty?"

Age is about the only thing in life that we get without trying.

One of the most important ingredients of happiness is a poor memory. There are many things in life that I would like to forget, but how to have a good laugh isn't one of them!

Small people tell you why you can't achieve your dreams. Big people make you dream bigger. Be sure to take notice of what successful people are doing. And remember, they are just as human as you are, so if they can do it, you can too!

Renowned nineteenth-century composer Giuseppe Verdi always received great applause for his performances. Those who watched him closely said his eyes always traveled upward to the box where his tutor sat. He did not react to the applause until he could see if his teacher was applauding too. What good is the world's acclaim if our Heavenly Master is not pleased?

Anyone who learns from his or her mistakes is getting a fantastic education.

Learn from the mistakes made by others. You won't live long enough to make them all yourself.

—AUTHOR UNKNOWN

A mother of three teenagers solved the problem of their staying out too late. She ruled that the last one in on Saturday night had to fix Sunday breakfast for the whole family.
—PAUL L. POWERS

Our granddaughter Paige was getting lessons from her Aunt Paula on good manners. "Auntie, if I'm invited out to dinner, should I eat my pie with a fork?" she asked.

"Yes, you should," came the reply.

"Well," she said with a smile, "do you have a piece I can practice on?"

You know what they say, practice makes perfect—especially when it comes to pie!

How many times have we found ourselves making the same mistakes over and over? Can it be that we are just not paying enough attention to what we are doing?

If experience is the best teacher, many of us are poor pupils.

—AUTHOR UNKNOWN

Happiness is typically not an end in itself but, rather, the side effect of some other endeavor.

THE SOUL OF A CHILD

The soul of a child is the loveliest flower
That grows in the garden of God.
Its climb is from weakness to knowledge and
*   power*
To the sky from the clay and the clod.

To beauty and sweetness it grows under care,
Neglected, 'tis ragged and wild;
'Tis a plant that is tender but wondrously
*   rare—*
The sweet wistful soul of a child!

Be tender, a gardener, and give it its share
Of moisture, of warmth, and of light,
And let it not lack from thy painstaking care
To protect it from frost and from blight.

A glad day will come when its bloom shall
*   unfold*
In the sensitive soul of a child.

—MFP

The birthstones of October are opal and tourmaline. The opal comes in black, dark blue, and gray with streaks of red, pink, and bright green. Tourmaline, which also comes in a range of colors, is said to help improve circulation, relieve stress, increase mental alertness, and strengthen the immune system. The flower for the month is the calendula, or marigold. Usually vibrant orange, this flower symbolizes passion and creativity, as well as sacred affection, but it also represents grief, despair, and cruelty. October is one of my favorite months because of the beautiful bright colors of the maple leaves.

OCTOBER

The heart of the poem "Footprints" is in the narrator's dismay over seeing only a single set of footprints during troubled times in her life. For all of us, the troubled times are not only the most revealing benchmarks of our spiritual maturity but also the times that move us ahead to greater levels of understanding. It is exactly for this reason that God often seems so strangely silent in our difficult hours—he wants to see us use the faith we have developed and to reach a new level of trust in him. Ask the parent of any young adult—a parent who is silent is not the same as a parent who is absent.

How well do your closest companions know you? Do they know what the best day of your life was? If not, start the conversation by asking what their best day was. The conversation will likely be a blessing to both of you.

Happiness is something that comes into our lives through doors we don't even remember leaving open.

—ROSE LANE

If you are really looking to discover your purpose in life, be brave enough to do something creative. Often we suppress our creative side, thinking that it's just not good enough or that others might laugh at us. You came to earth with a purpose. Have you discovered what that purpose is?

For those who eagerly await the beginning of another hockey season each year, here is a quote from Wayne Gretzky, "The Great One":

You miss 100% of the shots that you don't take.

Among hockey fans, Wayne Gretzky is widely acknowledged to be the greatest to ever have played the game, and he gives thoughtful advice (although I'm sure that Mr. Gretzky knows who "The Great One" really is).

A person's character is revealed by what he or she does after failure.

All the flowers of tomorrow are in the seeds of today.

—AUTHOR UNKNOWN

Fools are not the ones who ask questions; they are those who refuse to ask questions when they have them.

There's one thing for which you should be abundantly thankful—that only you and God have all the facts about yourself.

—AUTHOR UNKNOWN

Much wisdom is found in questioning what we think we already know.

A wise old owl lived in an oak;
The more he saw, the less he spoke;
The less he spoke, the more he heard.
Why can't we be like that old bird?
                    —EDWARD HERSEY RICHARDS

7

OCTOBER

October is a time for the gathering of harvest;
and with the work of another year finished,
there is time for the cultivation
and enjoyment of friendships.

—MFP

So many things that exist do so because someone had the courage to dream they could be. I'm one of those people who keep a notepad and pen by my bedside so I can write down anything that comes to me in my dreams, if I still remember it in the morning. So go ahead and dream. Who knows what you will come up with!

10

OCTOBER

Let us all be thankful that there is still
*   sunshine,*
that we can glimpse the blue of the sky
and, in our onward way,
continue to look up.
Let us be thankful for friends
and kindly smiles and encouraging words.
This is a time for grateful thanksgiving!

—MFP

Our daughter has been home-schooling our grandchildren. During one of our visits, we were able to help with their math lessons.

Our grandson asked, "Nana, what's eighteen divided by three?"

My reply was "Six."

"What's thirty divided by two?" he went on.

"Fifteen. But Calvin, shouldn't you be figuring these out yourself?"

Looking up innocently from his book, he replied, "Nana, the book said it's OK to use any method."

The events of our lives are not nearly as important as what was in our hearts when they occurred.

Too often people hope for a magic key to open the doors to our dreams, without realizing that the magic key is already within them.

It is not in life's chances but in its choices that happiness lies.

Do not be deceived: God cannot be mocked. A man reaps what he sows.

—GALATIANS 6:7

The lines of dots that run up our wall
tell us our children are growing quite tall;
shoes that were large now squeeze their toes.
My, how quickly a little child grows.

More important than inches, or dots on the
*   wall,*
is increasing in wisdom; as Jesus grew tall,
he grew in favor with God and with man.
Will your children do this?
With your help they can!

—MFP

Too many pastors fail to realize what advertisers already know—our ears are good for only about twenty out of every thirty minutes.

The empty-pew problem is not solved when the pew is occupied by someone with a wandering mind.

—PAUL L. POWERS

Note on the wall in the reception room of a small-town doctor: "To avoid delay, please have all your symptoms listed and ready."

If you intend to call one day
to see someone you know,
I'd go today and cheer her up,
come rain or hail or snow.
If you should let the matter wait,
Another day or more
You might be just a day too late
Your friend may be no more.

—MFP

In striving to make a difference in a child's life, don't overlook the fact that it is usually several small things that collectively make a big difference.

Reasoning with a child is fine if you can reach the child's reason without destroying your own.

—JOHN MASON BROWN

Be not impatient. Think of God's great patience in his work with man through the ages to bring about "Peace on Earth and Heaven."

I love you because . . .
you're sweet and thoughtful and you are mine;
God gave you to me, and I am thine;
your love is far deeper than surface or time.

God is molding us together with his love
    sublime;
rough edges to share,
together God put us in his wisdom divine;
he destined together we'd work as one
and with your name I'd sign!

—MFP
WRITTEN ON JULY 13, 1965,
IN VERONA, ONTARIO,
ON MY HONEYMOON

19
OCTOBER

Rather than finding fault, find solutions.

CHOICES

Life is full of winding roads,
it's up to you to choose.
The flat lands may be easier,
but the hills . . . they have more views!

—JODY BERGSMA

Too many people overvalue what they are not, and undervalue what they are.

It isn't what you have in your pockets that makes you thankful, but what you have in your heart.

—AUTHOR UNKNOWN

21

OCTOBER

Making plans is important, but without action, plans are just wishful thinking.

Maybe you feel it hasn't been such a good year so far. There has been world strife, widespread flooding and devastation, forest fires, riots, terrorist attacks, wars, corruption in high places, rudeness, moral decline, and taxes, taxes, taxes.

But look again at the sunshine dispelling the clouds. You still have the greatest gift of all. You still have a belief in God . . . the one who created the light so you could see the wrongs and do something about them.

Oh, the comfort, the inexpressible comfort
of feeling safe with a person, having neither
to weigh thoughts nor measure words . . .
certain that a faithful hand will take and sift
them, keep what is worth keeping, and with
a breath of kindness blow the rest away.
—George Eliot

Every season, you can take stock of how you can make a difference in the world. I believe it is important to support your family, church, and church family, and to have a passion for showing the fruits of the spirit. I have a deep inner faith to sustain me.

DEAR MIDDLE CHILD

*I've always loved you best because you drew
      a tough*
*spot in our family and yet it made you
      stronger for it.*
*You cried less, had more patience, wore hand-
      me-downs at times,*
and never in your life did anything first.
But it only made you more special.
You were the one we relaxed with and realized
*that a dog could kiss you and you wouldn't
      get sick.*
*In fact, you were always bringing home strays
      even in grade school.*
*You could cross a street by yourself long before
      you were old enough.*
*However, motorists were not so concerned
      about you. You helped us*
*to understand that the world wouldn't
      collapse if you went to bed with dirty feet.*
*You were a tiny child of our busy, difficult,
      and unsettled years.*
*We didn't have to kiss and cuddle you as often,
      because you were so independent,*
*but without you, we would not have survived
      the tedium and routine*
that is marriage.
*You drew each end of our family together, and
      we love you.*
                         —CLARENCE HENRY FISHBACK

Believe in your community. Don't be afraid to pick up after yourself and others. The motto in Vancouver when you go to an outdoor celebration is "Pack it in and pack it out," meaning bring food in and take garbage home.

One of the hardest lessons for me to learn is that I have no control over what others do. I can control only my response to the actions of others.

If you don't like the way things are, don't complain—work to change them.

Most of us tend to begin living only once we realize our time on earth is short. Don't wait until your later years to come to this realization.

Is it your goal to leave the world a better place than you found it? It may be that you are accomplishing this by doing one large significant thing, or by doing a number of small things. There are many ways we can do something that lasts beyond our years; these are the things that bring us the most satisfaction while we are here.

Most people would rather be with someone they like than with someone who is right.

You will always have to make choices in life, and there are no guarantees as to which choice is right. When you can't easily make a decision, get out pen and paper and make a "pros and cons" list. And remember, deciding not to choose is also a choice.

The birthstone for November is the topaz. Topaz, which represents fidelity, can be found in shades of orange, yellow, honey, red, light green, pink, and blue. The flower of the month is the chrysanthemum, reminding us of compassion, cheerfulness, friendship, sensitivity, and secret love. When given, chrysanthemums mean, "You are a wonderful friend."

NOVEMBER

At the end of "Footprints,"
God whispers words of encouragement
to the narrator. And in my own life, I
typically find that when God speaks, it is
quietly, through situations or deep inner
impressions in my soul. To meditate on
God, we must find places of quiet without
the myriad distractions that usually cover
up the sounds in our souls. Only then can
we expect to discover his movement in our
hearts.

No matter how bad things get, there is always something that you can be grateful for. I had a friend who was miserable because she had really messed up a project at work. She asked me what she should do. I advised her to apologize to her boss and to say that she would do her best to fix the problem right away. Then I told her to cheer up and be grateful that she wasn't her boss!

Your worst days are never so bad that you are beyond the reach of God's grace. And your best days are never so good that you are beyond the need of God's grace.
　　　　　　　　　　　　　—JERRY BRIDGES

Isn't it wonderful to discover what others see in something that we may have missed?

One day, a piece of pure white onyx was brought to a lapidary. On examining it, the man discovered an ugly stain of iron rust across it. What could he do in order to use the stone? As he studied it, he had an idea for transforming it into something of sheer beauty. He formed the white part of the stone into a Grecian goddess, and used the the iron rust as a tiger skin robe. Thus, what had seemed like a flaw in the stone was worked into something that increased its beauty.

—AUTHOR UNKNOWN

It's a good thing we live only one day at a time. I couldn't bear messing up multiple days at once.

God didn't say life would be easy, but he did promise he would be with you every step of the way.

—JOHN BALLARD

It's November, when children's coats flap against the first whispers of winter, and the world curls round itself to sleep in gratefulness and peace.

This day is mine to mar or make.
God, keep me strong and true.
Let me no erring bypath take,
no doubtful action do.
Let all I meet along the way speak well of me
*   tonight.*
I would not have the humblest say I'd hurt
*   them by a slight.*
Grant me when the setting sun
this fleeting day shall end,
that I rejoice over something done,
be richer by a friend.
Let there be something true and fine,
when night slips down to tell,
that I have lived this day of mine,
not selfishly, but well.

—MFP

When I am disappointed by the behavior of people from whom I expect more, I try to remember that just because we fall short of a way of life to which we aspire doesn't mean we shouldn't continue striving for it.

One Sunday, a little girl was given two quarters—one for the collection plate and another to spend as she wished. On her way to Sunday school, the girl dropped one of the coins, which rolled over the curb and disappeared into the storm sewer. The little girl looked through the grate into the watery depths and said sadly, "Well, there goes God's quarter."

—DOROTHY STOUFFER

It's hard to improve on bumper-sticker theology, but sometimes it's necessary. I saw a sticker the other day that read, "God said it, I believe it, and that settles it!" But it really should say, "If God says it, it's true, whether anybody believes it or not."

When my husband and I first married, bumper stickers were all the rage. Wanting to be with the "in crowd," many people had bumper stickers that read "Honk if you love Jesus." One day as we were driving we saw one of those stickers and gently beeped our horn as we passed by, only to see the driver shake his fist at us. After that, we decided the trend was just not for us!

8

NOVEMBER

Despite the fact that we all know death is a natural part of life, our grief at the departure is as much from the loss of a future we had imagined as it is from the loss itself.

I've touch'd the highest point of all my
  greatness,
And from that full meridian of my glory
I haste now to my setting. I shall fall,
Like a bright exhalation in the evening
And no man see me more.
                    —WILLIAM SHAKESPEARE,
                         Henry VIII

I have always been interested in quilts and quilting. My mother was a seamstress, and many of her friends were quilt makers. Whenever one of the family was planning to marry, quilters would sew up a quilt as a wedding gift. My husband and I received one of these quilts, which we still have today.

My friend and her husband send out quilting projects to people around the world. They even invited my husband and me to a stage play called *The Quilters*. This play offered great insight into Canadian history and an appreciation for the challenge of working to make life easier for our children and grandchildren.

It is a fundamental problem that we often mistake the inflexible person for a person of strength. The person whose opinions cannot be changed regardless of truth is no one to admire. But the one who can hold his or her tongue while staggering under the weight of a righteous cause—this is the one who is strong.

A moment of silence today is really not very much to ask. Please pray for all of our soldiers and their families.

IN FLANDERS FIELDS

In Flanders Fields the poppies blow
Between the crosses, row on row,
That mark our place; and in the sky
The larks, still bravely singing, fly
Scarce heard amid the guns below.

We are the Dead. Short days ago
We lived, felt dawn, saw sunset glow,
Loved and were loved, and now we lie
In Flanders Fields.

Take up our quarrel with the foe:
To you from failing hands we throw
The torch; be yours to hold it high.
If ye break faith with us who die
We shall not sleep, though poppies grow
In Flanders Fields.

—JOHN MCCRAE

When we die, the things we have kept to ourselves die with us. Only what we have done for others can live on.

The Happiness Box represents the love of a little boy for his cousin—a love that distance could not hinder. This little boy had nothing to give his cousin except an empty box. So he decorated it and filled it with love, joy, understanding, and peace. He gave it to his cousin, who cherished it greatly.

As the cousins grew older, they began to encounter the sadness, discouragement, and lack of understanding that is so often a part of this world. But the second cousin found life especially trying, until one day he remembered the Happiness Box. Pulling it from a forgotten corner, he opened it and found it still housed joy, understanding, peace, and, above all, love.

—ADAPTED BY PAUL L. POWERS FROM THE TRUE STORY OF THE HAPPINESS BOX

Virtue is not something we can develop in isolation. We must be among others to grow in its practice.

Those who hide the truth by obscuring language are guilty of far more than lying; they are guilty of violating others and sowing mistrust and suspicion.

A chrysanthemum by any other name would be easier to spell.

—AUTHOR UNKNOWN

Don't underestimate yourself. Some of the world's greatest leaders have suffered self-doubt at times. But those who have been the most successful have looked beyond their doubts and fears to see the greater good and have gone on to do it. Fear will get you nowhere; faith will move you forward.

Afriend needs you neither to lead or follow, only to walk beside.

Real friends are those who, when you've made a fool of yourself, don't feel that you've done a permanent job.

—ERWIN T. RANDALL

18

NOVEMBER

Children have few expectations of adults, but one is this—if you ask for their time, you better show up with a good story.

I cannot tell how the truth may be;
I say the tale as 'twas said to me.
—Sir Walter Scott

A truth, said in a timely manner, is more powerful against the injustice of a liar than the strongest prison.

Does a man speak foolishly?
Suffer him gladly, for you are wise.
Does he speak erroneously?
Stop such a man's mouth with sound words
    that cannot be gainsaid.
Does he speak truly?
Rejoice in the truth.

—SIR OLIVER CROMWELL

19
NOVEMBER

It's so much easier to dwell on the evils that have occurred in our lives and overlook the blessings. Today forget the evils and dwell on the blessings.

Bitterness is self-cannibalism.
          —HEATHER KAITLYN BARCLAY

*I would maintain that thanks are the highest
form of thought, and that gratitude is
happiness doubled by wonder.*
          —G. K. CHESTERTON

21

NOVEMBER

When you lie down to sleep tonight, go to sleep being thankful without hoping for more.

Money may not be everything, but it does keep you in touch with your children.
—ATTRIBUTED TO GREY OWL

I'd rather keep my mouth shut when I don't have anything meaningful to say and risk people thinking I am weak than open my mouth and have them think I am rude.

23

NOVEMBER

Our greatest unhappiness comes from our inability to be content with what we have.

I once heard a comment that I have weighed over and over again in my mind, and the more I consider it the more true it seems. Whatever you face in life, always choose the way that appears most difficult; it will typically be the best decision in the long run.

If our ancestors saw how we memorialize their accomplishments through our holidays, would they be pleased? The worst thing about a holiday is that the next day is not a holiday.

What are the best lessons you have ever learned—lessons from school, lessons from your parents, or lessons from real-life experiences? Sometimes real-life experiences can be the hardest and cause us the most grief. But there is nothing better than experience to teach us the lessons that really make us better, smarter, and stronger.

Many people have discovered their most valuable talents in times of adversity that they would have avoided if they could have.

Arguing is a form of arrogance—it denies the very real possibility that you may be wrong. Worse, it steals from others the acknowledgment that they may be right.

Sabrina fair,
listen where thou art sitting
under the glassy, cool, translucent wave,
in twisted braids of lilies knitting
the loose train of amber-dropping hair;
listen for dear honor's sake,
goddess of the silver lake,
listen and save.

—JOHN MILTON

A solid character is something that takes a lot of effort to build. It is not something that you are born with.

Be more concerned with your character than with your reputation. Your character is what you really are, while your reputation is merely what others think you are.

—DALE CARNEGIE

The quickest way to find common ground with another person is to laugh at something you both find humorous.

If you are tired of being hassled by unreasonable parents, now is the time for action. Leave home and pay your own way while you still know everything!
—MEL JOHNSON

The gemstone for the month of December is the blue topaz. The flowers celebrated during this month are hollies and poinsettias, or in some countries, narcissus and orchids. The meaning we derive from these flowers is reassurance, celebration, success, wealth, and formality.

DECEMBER

Every crisis, whether big or small, focuses our attention on the negative aspects in our lives and makes us forget the positives. In "Footprints," the narrator tries to place some sort of blame for the difficult times in her life and wonders why someone who could do something about her difficulties has chosen not to. But the wonderful thing about God is that he doesn't chastise us or get angry at our questions, even when they reveal our own lack of appreciation for all he has done. Instead, he gently reassures us that, regardless of our lack of trust, he is with us all the time whether we realize it or not.

In a world that is sorely lacking in empathy, I find that giving affection is one thing everyone appreciates.

A hug is a perfect gift—one size fits all, and nobody minds if you exchange it.
—IVERN BALL

There is no way to bring glory to yourself without crossing the bridge to arrogance. To receive glory, it must be others who see it and recognize you for it.

Glory to God in the highest, and on earth peace to men on whom his favor rests.

—LUKE 2:14

3 DECEMBER

Thinking about Christmas? I recently heard someone say that what she liked about Christmas was that you can make people forget the past with a present. Have you started your list?

Since I believe in God, the Christmas season is even more special and meaningful for me and my family. It helps to keep my life in balance. I have heard that the worst possible moment for an atheist is when he or she feels grateful and has no one to thank.

Any time you desire change, remember that it must come from you. The things around us cannot change, nor can we force others to change.

The significance of things and events comes only from our imposition or acceptance of what they stand for. This Christmas, create a new ritual—even if it is only for yourself—that will allow you to step away from the holiday madness and appreciate why we put ourselves through it every year.

It's not that some people have discipline and others do not; it's just that some people are ready to make positive changes while others are not.

God taught mankind on that first Christmas day
What 'twas to be a man; to give, not take;
To serve, not rule; to nourish, not devour;
To help, not crush; if need, to die, not live.
                                            —CHARLES KINGSLEY

Without friendship, a gift is just a kind of marketing.

Christmas is a time when everybody wants his past forgotten and his present remembered.
—PHYLLIS DILLER

9 DECEMBER

Both our niece and our granddaughter celebrate today as their birthday. It is always a special occasion.

One year, our grandchildren planned and prepared a lovely birthday party for me in California. It was a surprise "super sleuth" party and fun for all! Our three-year-old granddaughter, Corinna, said to me at dessert time, "Nana, do you want a cupcake? I made them myself with mummy's help." I tasted one and said, "Yum, yum. They're delicious. How did you get this icing so smooth?" She looked at me with her big blue eyes and said, "Oh, I licked them."

Grandparenthood is wonderful, since it is half the work and twice the fun!

Nothing is so old that we cannot learn from it.

All those things which are now held to be the greatest antiquity were at one time new; and what we today hold up by example will rank hereafter as a precedent.

—Tacitus

One of life's greatest secrets is that regardless of how old we are, we are nearly the person we have always been. Our bodies change, but our souls do not.

The daisy, by the shadow that it casts,
Protects the ling'ring dewdrop from the sun.
—WILLIAM WORDSWORTH

It is the season of shared meals and parties. Keep in mind the importance of meals in relationships: Take neither the friendship nor the communal sharing for granted.

14

DECEMBER

Are you a junk collector? We all have the habit of keeping things we no longer need. There's nothing more frustrating than hanging on to something for years on the chance that one day we'll use it, finally throwing it out, and immediately afterward needing it. But honestly, how many times does that happen? Clutter can slow us down and make us less organized. There are many great organizations that recycle or resell just about anything; so don't be afraid to pass on items to them. If you really need something you got rid of, there's a good chance that you'll find the item again at a thrift store for a nominal cost.

Homelessness is one of the saddest plagues of our time. Having no home to go to means having a lack of safety. But it also is a spiritual risk. The homeless are on a path to nowhere, filled with emptiness, surrounded by many, cared about by few.

A palace without affection is a poor hovel, and the meanest hut with love in it is a palace for the soul.

—ROBERT INGERSOLL

I have a very special friend by the name of Joy, and each year I try to search for a treasure with something appropriate that uses her name. Last year I found a fireplace stocking holder with Swarovski crystals spelling out the word *Joy*.

No joy in nature is so sublimely affecting as the joy of a mother at the good fortune of her child.

—JEAN PAUL RICHTER

A faithful friend is indeed a strong defense; and she that hath found such a one hath found a treasure.

—PARAPHRASE FROM SIRACH 6:14

Charity and generosity are not the same thing. Giving a token that costs us little is charity; it helps another but requires little sacrifice. Generosity is charity grown exponentially; it is extravagant charity.

18

DECEMBER

I hope the Christmas star will shine
your house within,
for love and wonder, joy untold,
will then begin;
and miracles will be for you
a part of life the whole year through.
                    —HEATHER MACGREGOR

We can never repay our parents for what they have done for us. We pass down to our children the goodness we owe our parents. Those without children pass it on to humanity in general.

19

DECEMBER

have learned that in most cases I cannot control the situation I am in. My only choice is to be happy in it or not.

Everyone is looking for something, even when he or she does not understand the search.

Every great or original writer, in proportion as he is great or original, must himself create the taste by which he is to be relished.
—WILLIAM WORDSWORTH

Every time I see a Christmas tree twinkling, I remember going out with my brothers and my sister on our sleigh to cut down a tree from our farm. Mum would have hot apple cider, hot chocolate, and popcorn ready when we returned. We would make paper dolls (origami style) and popcorn strands, and decorate the tree with these as well as with tinsel and colored glass balls. Then we would string fairy lights and various colored bubbling lights around the branches and make sure there was lots of water in the tree stand. Finally it was time to switch on the lights and enjoy a taffy pull.

Memories of today are the treasures of tomorrow.

Keeping Christmas is good, but sharing it with others is much better. The best Christmas gift of all is the presence of happy family members all wrapped up in one another. The *way* you spend Christmas is far more important than *how much* you spend at Christmas.

Quiet evening,
blissful hour.
Work is done,
shadows lower,
night is nigh.
Sweet repose,
Thoughts ascend
to God
who knows.

—HEATHER MacGREGOR

23

DECEMBER

Christmas Eve was always a special evening of the year. Our family tradition was to sing carols at the hospital and nursing homes as well as at our neighbors' houses. No matter how cold it was, we would stand outside each house and sing a few carols, and the people would love it and want us to keep singing. I played the accordion and my friend played the trumpet. The music cheered people and reflected the true kindness and goodwill of the season. When we returned home, we would listen to Charles Dickens' *A Christmas Carol* on the radio with our parents and help with the final gift wrapping.

Some people come into our lives
    and quickly go;
Some stay for a while and leave
    footprints on our hearts;
And we are never the same.

—MFP

Christmas in my childhood home was a magical day. We breakfasted on pancakes with whipped cream, read the Christmas story, and sang carols. Later, we would enjoy a wonderful dinner, then share the story of *Silent Night, Holy Night.*

There are several versions of how this carol originated. One says that John the woodchopper invited Pastor Mohr to see his new baby. When the pastor arrived after a long trek up into the hills, he discovered a beautiful scene: a stream of moonlight beaming through the window, encircling the mother and child.

On his way home, Mohr composed the poem, inspired by the scene in the cabin on that still, peaceful night. The next day, he gave the verses to his friend, the organist Franz Gruber, to set to music. The result is the carol that we sing today.

Merry Christmas to you!

But the good angel said to them, "Do not be afraid. I bring you good news of great joy that will be for all the people. Today in the town of David a Saviour has been born to you; he is Christ the Lord.

—LUKE 2:10–11

In Canada, we have designated the day after Christmas as Boxing Day. It is a day when people can get great bargains on leftover Christmas stock and return gifts that for some reason or other are unsuitable. One year, I had a few items I wanted to return, but I found the lineups so long and everyone so discontented and discouraged that I decided Boxing Day would not become a special day for me. When I finally finished my returns, I wanted to have a cup of tea with my daughters and friends, but there was no room in any of the coffee shops to sit down and relax. Many other shoppers just wanted a quiet spot to enjoy a cozy talk by the fireside, the laughter of little children, or an intimate moment with a friend. Often, people are completely exhausted after Christmas and just need to chill out with a friend or a loved one.

This is an excellent day to go for a walk, enjoy a hot chocolate, share a laugh, or spend a moment with some of the people in our lives for whom we may have not had much time over the Christmas season. Maybe we should rename the day "Friendship Day."

I often find myself singing or humming this carol to myself, even after Christmas. Maybe it's because there is just so much hustle and bustle leading up to Christmas that it's not until after all of the gifts are opened and the turkey and fixings are eaten that we can actually once again enjoy a silent night!

Silent night, holy night!
All is calm, all is bright.
Round yon Virgin, Mother and Child.
Holy infant so tender and mild,
Sleep in heavenly peace,
Sleep in heavenly peace.

Silent night, holy night!
Shepherds quake at the sight.
Glories stream from heaven afar
Heavenly hosts sing Alleluia,
Christ the Savior is born!
Christ the Savior is born.

Silent night, holy night!
Son of God love's pure light.
Radiant beams from Thy holy face
With the dawn of redeeming grace,
Jesus, Lord at Thy birth.
Jesus, Lord at Thy birth.

—JOSEPH MOHR

Many will say that you should start the day with some deep breathing to promote physical and mental well-being. So take a deep breath and surrender all of your fears, worries, and praise to the Almighty, and he will give you clarity and direction.

THE MEANING OF PRAYER

A breath of prayer in the morning
means a day of blessing sure.
A breath of prayer in the evening
means a night of rest secure.
A breath of prayer in our weakness
means the clasp of a Mighty hand,
A breath of prayer when we are lonely
means someone to understand.
A breath of prayer in our sorrows
means comfort, peace and rest.
A breath of prayer in our doubting
assures us the Lord knows best.
A breath of prayer in rejoicing
gives joy and added delight.
For they that remember God's goodness
go singing far into the night.
There is never a year or a season
that prayer may not bless every hour
And never a soul need be helpless
when linked with God's infinite power.

—AUTHOR UNKNOWN

Here is a poem that's easier said than done.

When we throw out
the Christmas tree
in the new year,
we should be careful
not to throw out
the Christmas spirit
with it.

—HEATHER KAITLYN BARCLAY

We often feel sad once all of the decorations are put away, and it's sometimes difficult to keep our spirits up and feel positive. One thing that may help is to put the decorations away over a period of a few weeks so that the place doesn't seem so bare all of a sudden. Or it can be a great time to hang up some new pictures of family members or loved ones that will bring a smile to your face or fond memories to mind.

Oh, to be content. All year long, we work so hard so that we can buy more things that we rarely use. Think back over the year about all of the things you bought, how much time it took you to earn the money to buy these items, and how much use you are really getting out of them. I can think of a lot of things that I don't need that I shouldn't have bought in the first place. Now think about something that you have that brings you real joy and contentment. It might be something that you didn't even buy or something that doesn't have any monetary value; treasure it, you are blessed.

A GRACE BEFORE DINNER

O thou who kindly dost provide
For every creature's want
We bless Thee, God of Nature wide,
For all Thy goodness lent.
And, if it pleases Thee, heavenly Guide,
May never worse be sent;
But, whether granted or denied,
Lord bless us with content.
Amen

—ROBERT BURNS

NEW YEAR

Before me lies a brand new year!
The path untrod, I do not fear.
For though the way be dark or light
My Father will guide my steps aright.
For I am His and He is mine
Oh, what a fellowship Divine.

The dying world so needs Thy Love
Oh Lord please send it from above.
Let it begin within my heart.
As in this New Year, with Thee I start.
And be Thou ever by my side
To strengthen, lead and be my Guide.

—PAUL L. POWERS

Once again, we are at the start of another year; how time flies. This is an exciting time of new beginnings, fresh starts, and promises made to ourselves and to others. I hope that as I leave you now, you will pass this book on to a friend or start over and read each entry again. I sincerely hope that these thoughts have inspired you and lifted your spirits when you needed it most.

Remember that anything can be accomplished if you trust in God and put your mind to it. Just take things one step at a time and make some new footprints— hopefully you will soon see that the footprints of others who have done good work cross paths with yours!

1 JANUARY